PHILOSOPHY OF PREDICTION AND CAPITALISM

MARTINUS NIJHOFF PHILOSOPHY LIBRARY

VOLUME 20

For a complete list of volumes in this series see final page of the volume.

Philosophy of Prediction and Capitalism

by

Manfred S. Frings
DePaul University

1987 **MARTINUS NIJHOFF PUBLISHERS**
a member of the KLUWER ACADEMIC PUBLISHERS GROUP
DORDRECHT / BOSTON / LANCASTER

Distributors

for the United States and Canada: Kluwer Academic Publishers, P.O. Box 358, Accord Station, Hingham, MA 02018-0358, USA
for the UK and Ireland: Kluwer Academic Publishers, MTP Press Limited, Falcon House, Queen Square, Lancaster LA1 1RN, UK
for all other countries: Kluwer Academic Publishers Group, Distribution Center, P.O. Box 322, 3300 AH Dordrecht, The Netherlands

ISBN 90-247-3542-4

PRINTED IN THE NETHERLANDS

TO KARIN

ACKNOWLEDGEMENTS

This is to express profound gratitude to Mr. George Miller, Graduate Assistant, Department of Philosophy, DePaul University, for having aided me along the way with helpful suggestions and philosophical comments, as well as for overseeing and coordinating the printing of the text.

To Richard A. Yanikoski, Chairman of the University Research Council, DePaul University, I wish to express my gratitude for granting me a research leave so that I could put this book into its final form.

CONTENTS

INTRODUCTION 1

PART I THE THREE CHARACTERS OF ABSOLUTE TIME

a) The Coincidence of Meaning and Phase 13
b) The Distinction between Becoming and What Comes-To-Be 17
c) The Phenomenon of Transition 33

PART II THE IMPULSION OF LIFE

a) Ultimate Foundations of Organic and Inorganic Matter 40
b) Impulsion and Phantasy 48
c) The Factors of Reality and Ideality 56

PART III MIND AND THE GENESIS OF HUMAN IDEAS

a) Two Examples for the Genesis of Ideas in Greek Philosophy 62
b) Contemporary Conception of Ideas: The Essence of Pragmatism 66
c) The Essence of Pragmatic Truth: Functionalization 71
d) Idea as "Sketch": Introductory Comment 87

PART IV THE UNFINISHED IDEA OF MAN

a) Man's Self-Understanding as Sketch 92
b) Capitalism and the Concept of an Entity 100
c) Variations of the Functional Appearance of Entities and the Role of the Sketch 115
d) A Second Look at the Idea as Sketch and the Essence of Capitalism and Economics 126

NOTES 142

INTRODUCTION

There is little more than a decade left before the bells all over the world will be ringing in the first hour of the twenty-first century, which will surely be an era of highly advanced technology. Looking back on the century that we live in, one can realize that generations of people who have already lived in it for the better parts of their lives have begun to ask the same question that also every individual person thinks about when he is faced with the first signs of the end of his life. It is the question: "Why did everything in my life happen the way it did?" Or, "It would have been so easy to have channelled events into directions other than the way they went." Or, "Why, in all the world, is my life coming to an end as it does, or, why must all of us face this kind of end of our century?"

Whenever human beings take retrospective views of their lives and times - when they are faced with their own personal "fin du siecle" - there appears to be an increasing anxiety throughout the masses associated with a somber feeling of pessimism, which may even be mixed with a slight degree of fatalism.

There is quite another feeling with those persons who were born late in this century and who did not share all the events the older generation experienced. A younger generation has more feelings of expectation, optimism, and hope. This is frequently expressed in their view that things must never again be the way they had been and that they must be improved with a touch of idealism. The past, they hold, must once and for all be considered passe. For one must work for and toward the future, so that more justice among men will prevail. Overall, there appears to be less of a sense of history in this youthful retrospective type of looking at the past in favor of a more circumspect looking on the present, and on what ought to happen in the future.

Much as such phenomena among people accompany all passing generations at one time or another, philosophy must not be affected by them. It is true that these phenomena, too, are objects of philosophical study. For example, the question can be raised what roles the past, the present, and the future play among different age-groups or have played in one's own lifetime. But philosophy proper goes far beyond such questions, interesting as they are. For it tries to unravel the essence of time per se, and of being, thinking them "in one," so to speak. Yet, the philosopher, too, cannot cut himself off from his own present, his own relative past and future. They do affect, no matter how slightly, his own conceptualizations of time per se. Every philosopher is also subject to the zeitgeist he lives in.

In our century, philosophy has entered many relationships with other disciplines and vice versa. This has happened to an extent never known before. These complex, interdisciplinary relationships resulted in a very large number of "philosophies" oriented around one or more than one such specific discipline. Of course, this fragmentation and specialization within philosophy itself did not prevent philosophy proper, i.e., foundational thinking, from occurring. Philosophy did not go under vis a vis its own interdisciplinary compartmentalizations. But it did recede in the background of these and of everyday life. So did most major thinkers of our century, whose essential messages were almost buried behind the clamors of short-term specialized endeavors. One can find the argument today that Kant's "transcendental apperception," among many other foundational notions in philosophy, does not help us anymore to solve practical or social problems. Nor is it helpful, they say, in preventing poverty, predicting business trends, or prolonging or improving the quality of life. And it even seems justified to argue that the great thinkers of our time said very little about certain pressing issues of the kind, which one might have expected them to do.

There is, however, a strong counterpoint to this viewpoint. Philosophical thinking is slow paced. It often resembles a musical counterpoint on which all sounds and chords rest, and without which they would hang in the air, helplessly. This slow-pacedness of philosophical thinking does not, however, agree very well with the restless speed of our lives and present-day cravings for ever faster short-term solutions of all impending problems. A philosopher's thinking is markedly isolated in our age of speed. He cannot compete with the inventions made in the name of speed and expedient shortcuts. For, after all, we do not only develop speed-reading techniques, say, those that will aid us in reading a 200-page book in an hour or so; we even develop machinery doing extremely complex ratiocinations in only fractions of seconds. And while this process has entered into the human sciences as well, philosophy, nevertheless, must face the foundational problems such as the "origins" of the technologies concerned. Without knowledge of this origin, no technology can be understood in its nature. But philosophy can do this only in terms of thorough, slow-paced thought. It cannot be done by way of quick, operative solutions or with the aid of a computer. Philosophy is conversant with the very presence of all that is. Its true objects, as Socrates called them, are "insights," i.e., not changeable ratiocination.

The difference between philosophical thought, on the one hand, and discursive, quick thinking, on the other, amounts to a clash that is as old as philosophy itself. Socrates' life is a vivid testimony to this, as are the lives of some of the pre-Socratics, e.g., Anaxagoras. The discrepancy between philosophical thought and everyday opinion can even lead to the oblivion of a philosopher himself amid everyday human concerns; as a result of this, the direction that history will take after such a philosopher will have been changed. Concerning the thinking of time per se, Pseudo Dionysos Areopagita, among others, is a case in point. In such cases, philosophy, i.e., the love of insight-knowledge, falls victim to philodoxa, i.e., the ongoing affection for quick solutions and transient opinions. It has been said that the effectiveness of philosophical insights depends upon two historical factors for their survival: chance and destiny.

He who is serious about thinking proper, i.e., the thinking of insights that are universal and comparable to those of mathematics, insights, that one cannot have or entertain opinions about - such as two plus two is four -, has before him the difficult task of finding them or of reviving them insofar as they had been found earlier in history, but were forgotten. In the latter case, one is not interested in reviving the name of a past thinker. Fame is no category of thought; rather, such activity preserves what has been found of value, no matter how old the insight may be. It can even happen that an insight is found at a particular time and coincides with the same insight that was forgotten a long time ago. This pertains, for example, to a number of insights made during the Middle Ages which are held to be creations of modern times because they "fit" into present-day concerns. In this, the older writings fell victim to fortuitous events of their times, and are still buried in those of today.

Philosophy must not concern itself with what is only topical at a particular time. It would lose its historical orientation. True, philosophy has often been used in support of what is topical. Nietzsche was used by Fascists, Hegel by Marxists in this fashion. And they still are. Overemphasis on topical issues is always short-lived. But in philosophy proper, there is an element which, despite the said utilizations, destiny, short-lived topical issues, and chance factors, makes insights indifferent to transient concerns as are uninterruptedly brought up in various disciplines. To this testify both ancient insights, such as "there is something rather than nothing," or the "principle of contradiction," as well as relatively modern ones, such as "a negative value cannot be preferred over a positive one," or "human existence is historical." The element that easily survives all transiency is familiar to anyone entertaining undivided commitment to truth. It is the spiritual joy that accompanies all individual search for truth. In this search, the philosopher experiences a communion with his self; he experiences the silence of the gathering of his thought and the humility and thanksgiving for all that exists. Kant experienced this overwhelming joy in seeing "the stars above" and the "inner moral law" within him. This experience has been shared by the twenty or so great thinkers, at one time or another, independently of the different eras and zeitgeister they lived in.

It is precisely during this being drawn toward truth, toward the totality of the world, and perhaps God, that the philosopher feels to be "above" the historical situation of his own times, looking down on it as if from a bird's-eye view. But he seems to have been unsuccessful over the ages in carrying the message of what he thusly intuited into the philodoxic attitude prevailing in everyday life.

The above brief considerations are offered at the beginning of this study in order to make clear what its title, PHILOSOPHY OF PREDICTION AND CAPITALISM, is not supposed to mean. We are not engaged, as one could expect, in forming some opinions on how the future may look. Ontic "prognoses" made into the future as we find them in novels like "1984" or in present economic and technological prognoses made for the oncoming decade of 2020-30 presuppose that the future looks like a "box" to the prognosticator. Prognoses are made, taken out, and new ones again put in, and are similar to those made in weather forecasting. This type of concept of the future is both taken for granted and unexamined while prognoses are set. The same holds for all "fortune-telling" and "astrology." It is a clock-time future into which foretold events are artificially assigned specific periods for them to happen in. But clock-time is not the only time pertinent to the future. For example, clock-time future is already very different from the role the future plays in "prophecy." For the nature of prophecy possesses a direction of time opposite to the aforementioned clock-time prognoses. In a prophecy, the future is not only enunciated by the prophet during his own personal lifetime. Prophesied future comes "toward" man in a reverse direction. Its schema not only shows that the future lies ahead of the present, but a fortiori, that the future is effective back onto the present. In a certain sense, the prophesied future is made earlier than the present in which the prophesy is made by the prophet - that is why I used the term "enunciated." By contrast, in the future that is foretold, the present can even be left behind for the sake of establishing something after it that may not even belong to the present. This is sometimes the case in fortune-telling.

The philosophy of time, which has been developed so remarkably during this century, and which has played an important role in philosophical studies as it never did before, never tackled the essence of prophecy, probably because prophecy is not pertinent to the spirit of a technological age and to a highly organized society whose world view is predominantly horizontal. But it is a serious deficiency all the same. Our study will not take up time in prophecy, either. But it will provide some starting points toward understanding time in prophecy, but only in an indirect way.

What we are proposing, then, is something deeply connected with the above: before any predictions in whatever area and discipline can be made, one has to elucidate what type of time-experience is at hand while predictions are being made. And this time is, as we shall see, not clock-time, nor any time connected with calculation, but "absolute time" in a meaning to be strictly defined and explicated.

In what follows, a number of valuable insights concerning the essence of time in prediction have been incorporated from a thinker of the first half of our century, whom Ortega y Gasset, Heidegger, and many others, have expressely praised to have been the strongest philosophical force in Europe during the twenties. That man is Max Scheler. But, in nuce, our study goes beyond Scheler. We are, therefore, not concerned with a presentation of Scheler's philosophy. Instead, we shall, as the title now indicates for us, concentrate on two problems that affect us all: 1) the essence of time and 2) the essence of our era.

Max Scheler died in 1928 at the age of fifty-four. At the end of his life, there were two concepts in his thinking that are recognized even today to be cornerstones of his philosophy, but which also have played a major role in the history of philosophy in general: the concepts of mind and life, or more precisely, of "mind" and the essence of life, "impulsion" (Geist and Drang). A peripheral understanding of these concepts came down to us in the English translation of DIE STELLUNG DES MENSCHEN IM KOSMOS (MAN'S PLACE IN NATURE). This was a brief summary of a part of Scheler's unfinished PHILOSOPHICAL ANTHROPOLOGY. This fragmentary summary, and many more elucidations of the concepts of mind and life were based on lectures Scheler gave toward the end of his life. Indeed, an extended lecture tour upon invitations from Japan, China, and Russia, during which he wanted to elaborate on his philosophical anthropology, would have given us definite clues on the meaning of the concepts concerned. This lecture tour, planned to extend over a period of two to three years, had to be cancelled because of the increasing illness of Scheler's heart functions. He was also invited to deliver a keynote address at the 6th International Congress, September 1926, at Harvard University. He could not follow through with this invitation. This was unfortunate because Scheler was - and is - the only European thinker who recognized American Pragmatism as a viable and necessary way of philosophizing. He regarded Peirce and W. James highly, and called the latter a "genius." His contacts with American pragmatists would have been important at the time of his short and cometlike fame in that it would have given a warning signal to the general European belittling of pragmatism that still rings out in our own days.

The fact that the aforementioned concepts remained unexplained after Scheler's death brought with it a number of critiques of them. This pertained especially to the concept of "impulsion" (considered to be the essence of life) and, peripherally, reminiscent of Freud's "Id" or Bergson's elan vital. Overall, the critique failed to see Scheler's basic intentions in three respects:

1. It failed to see that impulsion is "vital

energy" that propels not only all organic functions, but also all psychic and mental factors. As such, it is, like physical forms of energy, not an "object" in space and time; rather, it constitutes them.

2. It failed to see that the mind is "powerless" without life or impulsion.

3. It failed to see that both mind and life (impulsion) are "temporal" phenomena having temporal interconnections, overlappings, and interpenetrations, all of which are conjoined with "absolute time."

We will look into these three aspects later on and discover that the unity of mind, life, and absolute time belongs to the essence of pragmatic truth and that this unity cannot be regarded as an "object" among others but only as a dynamic unity of temporal functionalization.

Having this in mind, our investigation will, we hope, provide a small step toward grasping the experience of time necessary and basic for an understanding of prognostications. Our contention is that a clarification of time experience during prognostications is necessary in all technological, political, economic processes in which predictions are made. Whereas our study cannot claim to have paved a definitive way toward the essence of predictive experiences of time, it does suggest that more work on the problem must be done in an age that increasingly calls for predictions, be it in the world of atoms or in outer space, or more immediately, in the region between the world of atoms and outer space, where we live our ordinary existences.

A few words should be added concerning what is called the "phenomenological movement," of which Scheler was a part for a limited time. We do so because Scheler considered his major work on American pragmatism, "Erkenntnis und Arbeit," as a "gate" to his metaphysics and the same is true for the function of phenomenology in his thought.

There are two common errors to be found in all (premature) assessments of Scheler's phenomenology:

1. What so many phenomenologists - even present-day phenomenologists - consider to be the essential

notion of this field, the ego, is for Scheler only an "object" and not an X constituting the world (Husserl). The ego can, indeed, change its "location," either in the direction of "person" or in the direction of the "lived body." Furthermore, what in Husserl is "consciousness-of" is tantamount in Scheler to the "becoming" of consciousness, and the latter has its foundation in the "being" of person. "Person" is an "ontological relation," reminiscent of what Heidegger later on called Dasein.

2. The notion of the "lived body," explained by Scheler as early as 1913, must not be disconnected from the roles and functions of human "drives" that are the condition for phenomenonological explanations of perception, a point stressed in "Erkenntnis und Arbeit."

Since our investigation will begin with an explanation of what absolute time is supposed to mean, it is helpful to remind ourselves briefly of the divergent views that philosophy presents on the nature of time. It will only take a few examples for us to see how incompatible philosophies and concepts of time have occurred since Aristotle. Let us for the sake of clarity include the notion of space:

1. Aristotle - the temporal and spatial characteristics are determinations of substance. Time and space are accidental of something that underlies them. Time is the measure of movement.

2. Newton - time and space are infinite beings in which things are; they are objective.

3. Kant - time and space are forms of inner and outer intuition; they are subjective.

4. Marx - time and space are the measures of work.

5. Husserl - time and space are constituted in consciousness and lived-body-consciousness (Leibbewusstsein).

6. Heidegger - temporality of Dasein is the foundation of spatiality (plus whatever Heidegger elucidated in his later writings).

7. Einstein - time and space form a four-dimensional manifold.

Already, such a superficial enumeration of the various conceptions of time shows us the enormous incompatibilities between them. Time is either seen as a measure of something moving or as something existing, e.g., as a subjective form of perception, a measure of work, as constitutive of consciousness, as belonging to the question of being, as a factor of relativity dependent on the motion of an observer. Can one be in more disagreement on the nature of time?

What did Scheler think of the nature of time? First of all, he was in agreement with only one of the above conceptions: with Einstein's. Second, he thought that all concepts of time, including Einstein's, failed to see one presupposition: the "self-activity" of an agent, no matter whether this agent is "mind," "life," "energy," "consciousness," "drives," or "God." For this reason, we must remember that time is no human phenomenon alone; it is a form of all self-activity or self-activation. Time, therefore, is an a priori form of life, of the "bios," which does not belong only to organisms, but also to their individual parts, down to cells, molecular and atomic components. In short, time is the form of self-activity and self-change. Or, to put it into a nutshell: "Without life, no time."

It has often been said that even already during his lifetime, Max Scheler was a most germinal thinker. Whereas his influence on particular thinkers of his own time and of later times is hard to determine objectively, his anticipation of fundamental issues that would govern the rest of this century can more easily be established. Let a few of these be mentioned here.

It is characteristic in the history of ideas that a certain idea or concept becomes a prevailing one through one particular thinker, but that, on the other hand, such a concept was one of widely spread discussion among many other people. Thus, it can be held that a particular thinker more articulated than invented an idea that later on would put a stamp on future times. This is certainly true with the concept of "life-world," which is found in ever so many philosophical writings today. This concept was already widely used in nineteenth century German academic circles. Scheler's teacher, R. Eucken, for instance, spoke of the "workaday world" in his lectures, and Scheler himself used the expression of the "natural view of the world." Later on, Heidegger spoke of "everydayness." The concept of the life-world - today so common, especially among Husserlian scholars - may not have become so topical without its prior, generally accepted usage.

More direct anticipation of Scheler's influence can be found, for instance, in what Heidegger called the "at-handedness" and "present-to-hand" character of entities. This distinction can be found in Scheler prior to Heidegger's own, independent explication of them. Moreover, Scheler recognized the significance of the "lived body" as distinct from the "object body" as early as 1913. But even his own research may well have been under the influence of lesser known people like P. Schilder and E. Jaensch, with whom the distinction conerned was part and parcel of understanding the embodied human being, a basic thought that was only much later richly developed by Merleau-Ponty.

Special mention must be made concerning the contemporary thought and how the "thou" is prior to the "ego," or how the "alter-ego" is prior to the "ego." This priority was spelled out as early as 1913 by Scheler, leading to the subordinated role also of the ego to the being of the person. This anticipated the same subordination of the ego and of consciousness we find in Heidegger's Dasein. Other anticipations can be seen in Habermas' use of three types of knowledge - which Scheler had elaborated on in much detail everywhere - or in the treatment of the roles of values found in P. Tillich, who knew Scheler personally, or in the anthropological writings of Theilhard de Chardin. Anyone familiar with Piaget will find Schelerian anticipations of structuralism in the text that follows.

These instances should not overstress Scheler's role in the formation of the central themes of the twentieth century; nor do I wish, however, to forgo the opportunity to point out what is only fair to mention. If I had incorporated in what follows secondary literature of this kind, too many digressions from the theme before us would have ensued. The lack of reference to secondary literature is, however, mostly conditioned by Scheler's own prediction made in 1926 concerning the ways our world will be going. His essay MAN IN THE ERA OF ADJUSTMENT is the only one I could find among thinkers of this century successfully dealing with a philosophical prognosis, especially with regard to a long overdue recognition of the mind of the East.

My own attempt to focus on the philosophical foundations of prediction itself should serve as a pointer to the potential significance that the nature of prediction has in pure philosophy inasmuch as predictability in relation to lived time is experienced by the individual human being and humanity as a whole.

M.S.F.
December 1986
DePaul University

PART I

THE THREE CHARACTERS OF ABSOLUTE TIME

a) The Coincidence of Meaning and Phases

Inasmuch as in the constitution of a human being both mind and life possess temporal functions, we must ask the question: what kind of time is involved in this function? The answer to this question is: absolute time. We, therefore, must first clarify the nature of absolute time and will then be able to clarify the notion of the function that occurs between mind and life.

In explaining absolute time, we make use of practical examples rather than availing ourselves of complex philosophical terminology and concepts. This will not only help us approach the phenomenon of absolute time rather quickly, but also in a clear manner, as is necessary for our investigation.

There was already a form, or an aspect, of absolute time involved while the reader read the previous pages. While reading, our minds and perceptions passed along the printed words: parts of sentences and complexes of various meanings were understood, partially understood, or not understood. While reading, one also listened to the sounds of the words in one's "sub-hearing," so to speak. In the act of reading, one does not think of what time it is or will be; rather, we are immersed in the reading of a text with its sequences of series and groups of meanings that are connected with each other. This state of affairs becomes transparently lucid as soon as we fail to understand what we are reading and reread what we just read. In this case, one asks the question, "What is that supposed to mean?" In this case of being interrupted, the aforementioned flux of reading along and with the words is lost. Of course, one can also interrupt the natural flux on purpose. In that case, one may be reading "literally," or "critically," as a politician or lawyer must read agreements. The natural reading is, however, different from critical reading. As far as the absolute time and its natural flux is concerned, reading is not different from speaking. While I am speaking, the words and complexes of word groups that are uttered, too, are in fluxes of sequences that are not measurable. As far as absolute time is concerned, then, the natural flux experience of speaking and reading are not different from one another because they are disconnected from artificial clock-time. And in this sense, the term "absolute" may be taken to mean that "absolute" time has been absolved from clock-time.

The flux of time just mentioned points to the first characteristic of absolute time. In it, all meanings that occur "coincide" with phases in which they "run off" while reading. Both meanings and phases are "one," or meanings "fill" their own phases. Whenever this happens, Scheler speaks of absolute time. It disintegrates only when we pay attention to, are observant or critical of, one or another meaning that occurs. What is most interesting, however, is the fact that this flux of absolute time, or of time "filled" with contents, happens no matter whether meanings are true or false, whether they are nonsensical or imaginary, as in the case of fairy tales read by children. Clearly, the common distinction made between false or true, bad or good, ugly or beautiful, etc., have no bearing at all on the flux of absolute time.

The experience of the time flux in which meanings and phases are in complete tandem with each other is not, however, altogether characteristic of human beings. On the contrary, human beings always have a penchant to separate the two, i.e., to artificially place meanings into periods of time other than the original conjunctions. As it is well known, this characterizes "objective" time or clock-time. In it, time is made an object of calculation, and the calendar is a means to simplify and organize this objectivity. One can "shift" meanings, say, of an appointment, over to days other than they were originally intended to be. It is this very fact, in essence, that distinguishes human beings from all other animals, no matter what Darwinists believe they can show us about the descendents of the species. In contrast to humans, all animals live in absolute time, and their contents of perception are inseparably conjoined with their respective phases, unless human beings are able to disconnect their contents such that the animal might "put off" something, say, its mating time. The human experience, however, appears to jump over its original, vital temporality occurring in conjunction and coincidence with meanings and phases. Humans orient themselves "in" calendar-time, which they tend to conceive as time per se. Calendars belong indeed to the earliest and most ingenious inventions that humans have ever made.

But calendar time remains to be nothing more than a box for human temporal specifications. Pure experience of time, i.e., the time that is separated from calendar time, is quite different from this. It does not allow of calendars or any other measurement, because it represents a pure "run off" of phases "with" which we experience the contents of our lives and experience. Even if a scientist, who is always dependent in his research on the measurability of time, would question the immeasurability of absolute time, he could not question the very flux of meanings running off while asking the question. Absolute time can never be "objectified" or even sufficiently explained. We are always in it, or better, "with" it. One can only approximate its nature, including our own approximations here, because all experiences remain, at bottom, conjoined with it.

We can go one step further. Even when I have a discussion with a friend, the meanings involved are coincidental with the phases running off between us. We can call this "We-Time," or "Social Time" as Scheler did. And it is not only all groups that share absolute time of their historical phases; indeed, all history itself has this quality, before we look at history in a critical or objective way. Whenever the historian focuses on a particular event and its meaning, he must separate the latter from its original conjunction with phases in which these meanings have occurred. A historian separates them in order to locate the causes for this or that event. But the original intentions in the meaning get at least partially lost whenever we disconnect phases from their meanings. Original meanings, whatever they are or have been, occur only during the phases to which they belong.

The very seat, therefore, of any hermeneutics are the phases in absolute time in complete coincidence with the first occurrings of a meaning. All hermeneutics must keep "phase-meanings" in a constant view. For us, hermeneutics amounts to an investigation into absolute time, and not, primarily, to one of interpretation. All interpretation, too, occurs in absolute time. Therefore, it must seek the coincidence of a meaning and its respective phase, or the frame of phases of meanings, in which the meaning of the phase that is looked for has occurred.

It was stated that one cannot objectify, sufficiently describe, or observe absolute time (this includes the present attempt to get close to its nature through practical examples). We are so accustomed to looking at our watches - which outnumber the five billion or so people on this planet - that we tend to consider its measurable time as "the" time. We ask, for instance, the question: "What is the time?" But while we are asking this question, or say "Do I still have time to do this or that?" we are asking "out of" the flux of absolute time with its conjoined phase meanings. Measurable time is not the origin, but must be the very end point of a concept of time. Objective time is nothing more than a shadow that absolute time casts on us. Human beings live mostly in this shadow. Plants and animals do not live in this shadow of objectified time, but only within the experience of self-activity - if this can be called an "experience" at all. It is the self-activity of their own biological processes and perception, of their growth, of tropisms in plants, etc. We are including plants in our examples because in their own self-activity of growing they must have a vague phantasy that is not yet drive-related as it is in animals, and, therefore, can be considered a pure manifestation of the essence of life's self-activity.

It is not easy to hold the coincidence of phase and meaning in view because such holding in view itself possesses the character of absolute time. To grasp absolute time becomes even more difficult when one focuses only on processes in the activity of the mind which must, in essence, be of absolute time because the mind is a situs, as it were, of all meanings and contents. We will defer this consideration at this point in order to collect more data on absolute time itself.

The examples thus far given pertain to individual experiences such as reading as well as socio-historical considerations. But they do not suffice to lay bare the phenomenon of absolute time. The coincidence of meaning and phase is only one out of three characters of absolute time. The two others are: becoming and transition. We will now turn our analysis to these two.

b) The Distinction between Becoming and What Comes-To-Be

The following is designed to provide a number of characters of the concept of "becoming," which, like the coincidence of meaning and phase just discussed, is a form of absolute time.

In all what we said before, the "becoming" of something, and its opposite, the ceasing-to-be, was implied. While reading or speaking, meanings emerged; they came toward us; they were "becoming" in us. At the same time, however, they were also losing themselves in further backgrounds, passing away. In strict contrast to Husserl, Scheler conceived the whole of consciousness as under the aspect of "becoming" (Bewusstwerdung in contrast to Bewusstsein). All consciousness is a process of "becoming" toward what "will have become" at any time in terms of a more or less fixed meaning. All mental insights, ideas, concepts, contents, etc. are "becoming" along with their phases while they are, at the same time, also in the process of "un-becoming."

Let us look into the vital, or biological, processes in order to clarify further what has been said. A vital process, like the growth of a seed into a tree with both its branches and roots, is substantially different from a mechanical process. Vital motion of this kind must be distinguished from mechanical motion. Mechanical motion is determined by an end point, "terminus ad quem." The downward path of a rock falling on a pane of glass is determined by the law of gravity and follows the laws of classical physics. This is not the case in vital motion. The way a seed grows into a tree has no comparable determination. Rather, the motion is determined by its beginning point, "terminus a quo," its "inception." After its inception, self-motion has only tendencies. The branches and roots spread over the years without determinations of mechanical necessities or a determining terminus ad quem. Moreover, since vital motion departs from its a quo, it both spatializes and temporalizes itself, which is not the case with a falling rock. Vital motion is both spatialization and temporalization. For this reason, all vital motion "ages." In contrast to the rock, vital motion may be said to "conquer" its space and time. The falling rock falls "in" space and time, but in itself possesses neither space nor time.

In order to be fully able to understand this simultaneous becoming and un-becoming in self-motion, one would have to place oneself within the seed, rather than observe its growth before us. Only then could we be in the position to see the very difference between the pure vital self-becoming and un-becoming, on the one hand, and "what comes to be" of calendar time or mechanical, measurable motion. But we are so much conditioned by what we see with our eyes that we tend to confuse the pure vital becoming of the seed's growth into a tree with "what comes to be" of it. We say, for example, "It will take fourteen days before the plant will come out." But this calculation presupposes the self-temporalization and the very self-becoming of the process. In pure becoming, there are neither fourteen days, nor the square feet making up the garden in which the plant grows. The becoming of the plant has neither objective time, nor space. They are phenomena only in our own perception of it.

In addition, vital self-becoming must be characterized by its "void," which has nothing to do with the empty "box" of a future into which forecasts are made. The vital void is "in" the tendency of the self-growth of the seed; or better, it is "with" its terminus a quo. By contrast, the mechanical motion of the falling rock has no "tendency." It has a fixed track on which it moves, as it were. The seed, however, is "in itself" a void into which it paradoxically is becoming, or which the self-growth fills out. The void is, in a certain sense, a potency, albeit not in the meaning that Aristotle gave, viz. as a property of a substance. Rather the seed "is" potency itself qua tendency of becoming. It is a vital center, having auto-kinetic energy of its own that is different from all forms of physical energy, such as heat, motion-, position-, atomic-, gravitational or electric energy. The distinction made between vital and physical energy was typical for the later Scheler. It is, indeed, a justified distinction in his metaphysics, much as the distinction is still under investigation today and not clarified.

For if we take another look at the seed growing into a tree, the growing activity is, on the one hand, subject to the pulls of gravity, but on the other, it defies it. The seed and the young tree grow against gravity both in the upward vertical directions of the branches, etc. and the downward directions of the roots. For the roots reach "deeper" in their growing downward than the gravity allows. Hence, already plant life is enmeshed in two forms of energy, physical and vital energy. And one can see that Scheler scored a strong point in distinquishing in his "meta-physics" and "meta-biology" "force-centers" or "field-forces," on the one hand, and "vital forces," on the other. Possible interactions among force-centers and vital forces was a major area of his scientific research.

Vital energy of life-centers is also to be distinquished from force-centers or field- forces in that it cannot be measured. Vital energy seems to be of a "psychoid" character that cannot be associated with atomic energy so readily, much as it has been under discussion with people like Schrodinger. One must also keep in mind, though, that the atomic processes are not subject to the laws of classical mechanics, but to statistical laws only. They do not follow any hidden causality that even Max Planck sometimes assumed there to be behind all statistics. Causality of classical mechanics has no place in biology. Scheler also suspected that the physical force-centers and biological life-centers are not at all so different from one another as it is suggested by our everday experiences and visual perception of what is animate or inanimate. Indeed, he tried to demonstrate that both the vital and force-centers are two sides of one and the same principle underlying both life and inanimate matter. It is the principle at the same time that posits the reality of both: impulsion. Although impulsion must be taken first in the sense of a force in the life of any organism and its parts down to cells and chromosomes, etc., it is conceived, nevertheless, as that X which posits the reality of both vital and inanimate nature with their respective motion and change. Thus, the principle of impulsion underlying life and inanimate nature is indifferent to this distinction. Organic and inorganic nature are only two sides of the same process: the self-becoming in absolute time of universal impulsion. This point will prove to be of importance to us later on. For we will see that history is characterized by impulsive becoming of its own kind situated in the sub- and pre-conscious "becoming" of human drives, which may exercise deeply rooted or even concealed effects on the very becoming of the coming-to-be of a future that is objectively projected or prognosticated in calculating fashions.

It is for this reason that we take a second look at the pure self-becoming, viz. as it manifests itself in human drives.

The number of human drives is still under debate,

but there seem to be anywhere between twenty and twenty-five of them, among them, for example, the drives of propagation, of power or the drive of dying, of acquiring, or sleeping, of hoarding and collecting, the drive to live, etc. For our purposes, we will focus on the drive of nutrition. In addition to the procreative and power drive, the nutritive drive belongs to the main drives.

All drives are pre-conscious, i.e., their occurrences happen prior to our awareness of them. As soon as we realize that we are hungry or begin to be hungry, the nutritive drive had already been welling up under the bottom of our consciousness and knocked, as it were, at it. Our becoming aware of being hungry was preceded by the "becoming" itself of the drive. The welling-up ran off prior to the feeling of hunger and of wanting to eat. Whatever wells up in this fashion has the character of self-temporalization. Welling up does not only occur in drives, however, but also in such experiences as awakening from narcosis, or during waking up in general. Even intellectual insights well up before they become "present" in the mind, as we shall see later.

All subconscious drives have their own subconscious objects: drive-objects. The correlation of a drive and its object pertains in the above example to the proper content of the nutritive drive toward which it refers itself. This content cannot be defined, let alone be named. One can say at least that the nutritive drive refers to a very vague content of nutrition in general, having no particular aspect to it. It is purely, phantasmic or generated in the drive itself with its own subconscious imagination or phantasy. It is only when the drive knocks at the bottom of our awareness and begins to send its message to it that the phantasmic image of "nutrition in general" becomes conceptualized and specified. But in essence, drive and drive-objects are "one" and united, just as in consciousness act and intentional referent are united. Neither can be without the other. Drives, too, have their intentionality existing between their object and self-moving drive activity. Strictly speaking, the indivisibility of the oneness of drive and its object must be considered itself as pure becoming, and it cannot be the case that objective time plays any role in drive-life.

This leads us to a first conclusion: all pure becoming is pre-temporal. Insofar as pure becoming can be found in plants, animals, or in vital energy in general; and insofar as it can be found in psychic, emotive, rational, personal, evolutionary, and cosmic processes, there must be pre-temporal becoming in all of them. We call this becoming "pure" becoming. The pre-temporality can, of course, lead over into our "conscious" time experience, and whatever was in the pre-temporal processes of pure becoming will become something more or less "fixed" in our awareness of it. This state of affairs is obvious in the example mentioned earlier, viz. that an insight, say, a mathematical one, "has" become something fixed after it was becoming in absolute time prior to the insight concerned. We sometimes express this even in everyday life, when we say: "It occurs to me that . . ."

All pure becoming possesses a property we do not find in inorganic objects. For all phases running off during self-becoming processes are at the same time "un-becoming." Hence, pure becoming and un-becoming are inseparable.

The simultaneous becoming and un-becoming of what has become is much more obvious than we tend to think it is. In our everyday experience, we are continuously exposed to both the emergence of thousands of things around us and to their disappearance from our perception. In this, there is no causality involved that would "cause" this to happen. Indeed, we do not think of causes at all when we suddenly see, say, a cup on the table we did not see there earlier. The cup's appearance is, however, like a matter-of-course to us; we take for granted its emergence in our perception without questioning it. It is "natural" that the cup is there now. At any moment during our lives, Scheler contends, we experience the emergence of new and ever new things around us in this fashion while others disappear without our taking notice of them. They fall "into" the field of our perception - out of the blue, as it were - only to sink back and recede into relative nothingness. This occurs at a fast speed. This character of the noncausal becoming of things in our perception, their coming upon us and disappearing, must be sharply distinguished from something that "comes-to-be" as we find it in inorganic processes, such as the aforementioned falling rock. For the un-becoming of a phase of a process of growth, for instance, is "in" the becoming of it at any moment. At no time are becoming and un-becoming separated.

There are only two types of un-becoming in becoming:

1. Each phase is, on the one hand, itself becoming un-becoming or, depending how we look at it, un-becoming becoming.

2. One whole organism or the whole mind with its meanings, ideas, etc., is becoming toward its final end. That is, the final stage, although both becoming and un-becoming, "un-becomes" in the end.

Every type of self-activity or self-becoming in absolute time possesses its coming-to-an-end, which, in itself, is not caused by anthing outside the process concerned - although it may, for example, because of accidents. All self-moving life goes in one direction: its coming-to-an-end, granted that all general life is constituted by the self-activity of vital energy: impulsion. Both aging (un-becoming) and death (coming-to-its-own-end) are "in" pure becoming. They do not have their origins in the objective coming-to-be. For pure becoming temporalizes itself, ages, and ceases-to-be (dies), whereas what is "coming-to-be" happens in objectified calendar time only. It has, therefore, often been stressed that inorganic things neither age nor die, unless they, too, are conceived under the aspect of resting in a cosmic, self-activating impulsion. If one assumes there to be such a universal impulsion as the bearer of both organic or inorganic matter, the world must be conceived as "organoid," or in a very wide sense of the term, as a becoming and un-becoming, organismic whole of absolute time.

What we have thus far gathered remains on the surface of what we are about to show later. But at this point it can already be seen that, if the preceding is only partially true or valid, absolute time must bear heavily on the history and future of mankind.

On the basis of the above, one can ask a number of questions that have been raised since times of yore, but which would appear in a novel light for us; questions, that is, that are pursued indirectly or directly by researchers of no matter which science. Such questions include: "What is the present 'age' of mankind?" "Does mankind have an inherent ending, comparable to the inevitable death of every individual? In other words, is there a death of the species?" "Will mankind and human history die while the physical universe remains unaffected and continues to exist in the absence of the human mind that conceptualized it?" "How old is mankind with respect to absolute time?" Is the human species still budding, developing toward, say, an overman?" "Has present-day mankind reached its own mid-life crisis?" Is it the case that various civilizations age in terms of phases, rather than in terms of allocated periods?" "Do they age simultaneously?" "Is there 'simultaneity' at all in absolute time or among two or more individuals?" "Can it be held that so-called ancient civilizations, such as the Chinese and Egyptian ones, are as old as calendar time would suggest to us?" "Or, can it be the case that they are in absolute time still at the inception of growth?" "Does, by comparision, the so-called younger, western civilization already have "less" of a future than is believed or science fiction has suggested to us?"

These questions cannot be remotely answered in terms of objective, measurable time. Indeed, absolute becoming must possess a futurity of its own, and that is radically distinct from a calculable future. As far as absolute time is concerned, the "future" of humanity is at least in a large part indifferent to calendar time. In absolute becoming, the future is no "box" in which events happen or into which they are forecast, nor is our individual life such a box. From the viewpoint of absolute time, the future lies not in the year 3000, let alone did it happen in 1984. Rather, absolute futurity must be contained in every phase of individual and collective historical un-becoming becoming; that is, its direction is without dates. Dates and years are handy points of reference and orientation. They pertain to the "coming-to-be" or coming-about, whereas, as the form of the becoming of meanings, the phases of absolute time are their precondition.

For this reason, any theory of history that projects humanity on the plane of objective time with necessary goals that must be realized, i.e., any theory of history that, like the Marxist theory, wishes to predict the future of mankind into an objectified future determined by so-called historical laws, is complete nonsense. For such determinist theories overlook the fact that the becoming of history cannot be compared to the necessities and causalities of, say, the classical sciences of the nineteenth century. The becoming of every historical moment, as well as of history itself, is a process of self-temporalization whose phases unite with their respective historical contents of events, whereas in a calculated present, historical meanings of historical events and their phases are not united anymore, but only in the pure becoming of their present. The becoming of every historical moment, along with the becoming of every moment in one's individual life, does not allow of said box-concept into which we calculate, project, make plans, or wish to change the world.

In his lecture on Heraclitus, entitled THE INCEPTION OF WESTERN THINKING (HERACLITUS) given in 1943, Martin Heidegger made reference to the aforementioned "box-concept" that appears to be characteristic of our own age more than we may want to admit.[1] And he states that we even tend to consider every morning, noon, or evening as daily boxes into which we plan and project everything possible, and into which we pack as much as is efficiently possible. This line of everyday thinking is very convenient, and indeed, effective, because it lends itself to practical organization of all that we plan to do. But Heidegger at the same time ridicules this type of organizational thinking in terms of a pun using the German word beschränkt in two ways, viz. as meaning "furnished with cabinets," which is the literal meaning of the word - rarely used in German - and in the usual sense of "simplemindedness" or "limited intelligence." The gist of Heidegger's pun is much stronger, though it would compare in English to saying that modern man tends to put everything into a nutshell so that he has everything quickly ready and handy to him, and that in doing so, he does not see that this way of thinking drives society "nuts." For Heidegger, this means that man does not see into Being, and, instead, remains concerned with entities to be organized. For Scheler, this would mean something slightly different, but in essence, the same: man does not see the self-becoming of Being and, instead, sees only the coming-to-be of what occurs in objective time.

It was stated that history has phase-directions of absolute time. This was to indicate that history, in every one of its phases, possesses becoming and un-becoming with respect to contents and meanings. But both becoming and temporal un-becoming in absolute time are dimensions of general, absolute becoming. The seeds of all futurity must already be in the very becoming of what has become present now. And in the present that just now became, there are new seeds of becoming, having the direction toward what will again become a present, etc. Becoming and un-becoming are dimensions in absolute time, having nothing to do whatsoever with the conception of a future resembling a box into which one makes plans. The pre-temporal dimensions of "absolute" time have quite different layers of temporal fluxes than we would expect them to have when we are oriented in calendar time. These dimensions are self-temporalized. Scheler showed this to be the case in the human experience of time itself, which, of course, must be a prototype of aging and coming-to-an-end (death). Let us briefly show this.

Among the young generation of human beings, the

future is an open field without a horizon - or tendencies to have horizons - that would demarcate future events. Figuratively speaking, the young person or adolescent goes insouciantly to sea, challenging the forces of nature without expecting to confront the shores at the horizon that could terminate his ventures. If such shores come into view, he only uses them for a respite; then, it is back to sea again. His present is directed to the future, and the past is of little interest to him. But when he reaches middle age, the sphere of the future begins to contract; it begins to be demarcated by an inevitable horizon, while the past grows and grows from behind the present at any moment. Indeed, the past becomes more meaningful and weighty. It is, however, in between the contracting of the future and growing sphere of the past that the present becomes ever more "squeezed." In advanced years, the present is so "squeezed" that it does not have enough elbowroom for the possibilities left. In old age, the experience of time becomes petrified. The character of the contracting sphere of the future that continues to withdraw backward into the sphere of the present does not contain the capacity to experience more than what has been. For this important reason implicit in the experience of human aging, i.e., of a slow, inevitable un-becoming becoming, death is no concept derived from outside, observable experiences of the deaths of other persons; rather, death is contained in the very dynamic shifting of the spheres of the future, present, and past themselves, which are factors of the becoming and un-becoming of absolute time itself. This means that the direction of absolute time is toward un-becoming and complete self-ending. Or, the ending of absolute time in a human being lies in the direction of the tendency of absolute time.

On the basis of Scheler's analyses of the nature of aging and death, any prediction designed to provide a sketch of a becoming future must take into consideration the withdrawal of the sphere of the future back onto the present of a particular historical moment, as well as its degree of the future's contraction. Prediction must, inevitably, take into consideration the absolute age of the historical moment "in" which the prediction is attempted.

This would indicate for us the following: the determination of the temporality as becoming, i.e., the being of time, must be as important in prediction as is the determination of what is to come to be, or not. The reason why forecasters and experts in such areas as economics and meteorology are at times in unanimous agreement concerning what is about to happen but does not occur may well have its origin in the neglecting of the nature of absolute time. It was only recently that forecasters were unanimous in predicting that falling oil prices would boost the U.S. economy. Because of the high consumption of oil in the U.S., the benefits to oil consumers would overpower the damages to the domestic industry. As we now know, these forecasters were also unanimously wrong. Oil producers shut down many of their operations, and Texas and Louisiana came dangerously close to experiencing recessions. Forecasters not only disregarded the multiple effects on the economy coming from the always vocal groups and large groups of declining stocks, but also managed to overlook the very historical moment and its phases of the becoming and un-becoming of interdependent, global economic relations (there is no "national" economy anymore) in which, perhaps, "oil" has long seen its days, i.e., having a little futural horizon to itself in an increasingly sophisticated technology of energy. Criteria for the nature of the historical moment in which predictions are made are hard to find. It is even difficult to determine whether this moment may belong to a more youthful than an aging becoming of progressions of historical phases. One criterion, though, seems to be recognized in general, at least as far as the SOCIOLOGY OF KNOWLEDGE is concerned: increasing feelings of determination and mechanical world views point to an aging culture as is the same with the life of the individual in whose progressive age more fixations of views and outlooks are obvious. In any case, we can say that predictions that do incorporate the nature of phases of the self-becoming of historical moments and of their contents and if possible the degree of the contraction of futurity at hand, must be very different - if not closer to the truth - from prognoses made with calendar time, as we find them in economic or weather forecasting.

Since the shifting in absolute time of the dimension of future, present, and past is of special significance to our investigation, we want to graph this state of affairs so that we have it with us all along down our paths toward the possibilities of prediction. In the graph below, F stands for the shifting of the sphere of the future, P for the shifting of the sphere of the present, and PT for the shifting of the sphere of the past. Graphs, of course, always leave something to be desired in them. The term "youth" relates only to the first moments of a human being's experience; the term "age" refers to the last of the experiences before dying. "∞" signifies "infinite."

1. Youth $\quad$ P $\longrightarrow$ F ∞

PT $\leftarrow$ P $\longrightarrow$ F

2. Middle Age $\quad$ PT $\longleftarrow$ P $\longleftarrow$ F

PT $\longleftarrow$ P $\longleftarrow$ F

3. Age $\quad$ PT $\longleftarrow$ P

This graph of the shifts of the three dimensions of future, present, and past in absolute time serves to clarify the nature of absolute time: during the phases of increased aging of an individual, of a group, of a civilization or culture, or even of all humanity as such, the possibility to master at least to a certain extent, or get into some kind of control, of future events diminishes in proportion to the uncontrollability of the growing past, generating a growing determinism, mechanism, and even possible fatalism, along with the withdrawal of the sphere of the future toward an increasingly "squeezed" present. A global feeling of the uncontrolability and unmanageability of history would, on this basis, be an index for an aging humanity expressive of a pessimism of life in general. By contrast, a global feeling of indeterminism, of individualism, and of a spirit of adventure would be an index of the growing phases of becoming. In short, the distinction we had to make earlier between un-becoming becoming, on the one hand, and becoming un-becoming, on the other hand, now receives, in light of the shift of the dimensions or spheres in absolute time, its proper designation: youthfulness must be characterized by the becoming of phases that are at the same time already un-becoming, i.e., it must be characterized by "becoming un-becoming," whereas age must be characterized by the opposite, the general un-becoming of what is still becoming, i.e., as "un-becoming becoming." All of this must, of course, be intuited in absolute time; it cannot be taken in any sense of objectified, calculable clock-time.

But, more importantly, the graph signifies something else. The traditional view, according to which the past bestows onto the present indices for what should be done in the future, or indices of our learning from the past for the benefit of living better in the future, can only be taken in a conditional meaning. This is because the contracting sphere of the future, too, possesses its own effects with respect to the present. While it gradually withdraws toward the direction of the present, it restricts the originally vast numbers of future possibilities during youth; but in growing age, a few possibilities remain that, because of their small number, are all the more in bold relief to the aging mind. The increasing effects that a contracting future sphere has on the present can clearly be seen in the growing awareness, and at times semi-hysterical concern, for social security, or other sheltering social device.[2] Historically, this state of affairs would also support the fact that throughout all myths and religions it was the wise man (East), or the seer and prophet (West), who as an old human being is wise and seems to possess something more than human knowledge. But he was not "old" in terms of a larger number of accumulated birthdays. It is always at the end of his life, no matter how old he may be, that the prophet annunciates his eternal message in terms of the "latter" status of the shifts of absolute time in him. The prophet does not forecast the future; on the contrary, the contracted sphere of the future touches the present (P<--F), bestowing on it an everlasting historicity. It is thinkable that the only reliable predictability available to man lies in the reverse direction of time flowing from the contracting sphere of the future toward the prophet's present.

For us, it is, however, the converging effect onto the present of both past and future that is quintessential for the conceptualization of prediction. That is, we must look into the nature of a historical moment or event as such, which will give us further insights into absolute time.

There are two conceptualizations of a historical fact or event. They are the extremes within which all other interpretations of the nature of the historical fact are made. On the one hand, a historical fact or moment can be seen as a happening that is itself complete, and, on the other, it can be seen as something that is incomplete or open-ended.

All types of historical determinism, as, for example, classical Marxism, must regard a historical fact, say, Lincoln's Gettysburg address on November 19, 1863, or Caesar's crossing the Rubicon on January 15, 49 B.C., as "complete." It is regarded as a completed fact in the series and progressions of other historical determinations. According to this view, history possesses its own inner necessity, for instance, the necessity toward historical materialism leading to a socialist world communism.

There are also conceptualizations of the historical fact that are less determined. They are implicit in many stories of religious and mythological prophesy. The myth of Perseus shows that the fulfillment of the prophesy, viz. that Perseus will kill his grandfather (unknowingly) is not dependent on the long chain of adventures he goes through until the moment occurs when his discus hits his grandfather. All events between the oracle that prophesied and the killing could have taken place in many other ways than they did. There is enough freedom in between the beginning and end of the prophesy that warrants Perseus a free hand in whatever he is doing up to the fulfillment of the prophecy. An extreme determinist view, by contrast, must conceive every single historical moment as at least in part being necessary if such a theory wants to be taken seriously at all. It is well known how Lenin attacked both Einstein and Max Planck for their indeterminist scientific theories. To this day, historical determinism has not skirted its presuppositions.

The opposite of a determinist understanding of the historical fact is the idea of the incomplete historical fact. It is not only incomplete with regard to the endless possibilities of its interpretations made by later generations, but also in terms of its own nature: the historical fact is "in itself" incomplete as is also any of our own moments of living. This implies that any event could have turned out differently from what, in fact, it did. The life of every human being is open-ended, having no determinations except those that lie within the infinite possibilities of the one individual himself and that no other individual has. Scheler, along with many other historians in the early twentieth century, opted for the latter view. History, then, at any of its moments of predictions, possesses "open" tendencies originating in the terminus a quo of the becoming of every moment in which contents and phases become and un-become in absolute time prior to their transformation into objectified time. But the processes of all becoming and un-becoming in pre-temporal, absolute time must also possess transitions among each other that do not point to a determinist, causal track, but to the very open-endedness of any moment and its moments following.

c) The Phenomenon of Transition

During the previous discussions of the two aspects of the absolute time, the coincidence of meaning and phase, and pure self-becoming, we had been presupposing all along the third character of absolute time, transition, which may turn out to be the most important of all. It was necessary for us, however, to first look into both coincidence and self-becoming, in order to place the nature of transition in view. There is no question that all self-becoming implies the transition from any one point over to the next, and all transitions imply both becoming and un-becoming.

We know of the significance of transition since Heraclitus, who speaks of such transitions as holding between "sleep" and "being awake," between "life" and "death," "young" and "old."[3] Heraclitus maintained that throughout all transitions in the world going on from one term to another there is "the same." Traditionally, this has been interpreted to mean that, say, death and life, sleep or wakefulness, the way up or down, are the same, i.e., one tends to argue that the respective terms of transitions are the same. But this is often hard to think, unless one states that, say, life and death are two sides of "the same" in the sense that one side looks concave, the other convex, neither of which being able to hold its own without its opposite and thereby being the "same." As far as I can see, it has not yet been argued whether the Heraclitian notion of "the same" means the transition itself, which amounts to saying that being is, in essence, ever becoming transition. We cannot go into this possibility here, and must leave it for a later study.

There are, of course, many more transitions than the ones enunciated by Heraclitus. There were, for instance, transitions in reading this text, going from one meaning to another. There are transitions throughout the wellings of our drives that come and go; there are also the transitions from relative non-being, leading into the being of a thing as it occurs in the human perception of things emerging and disappearing.[4] All transitions, we can say, are characterized by becoming and un-becoming.

Like becoming, transition can function in terms of universal applications in reality. There are vital transitions, mental transitions, transitions occurring in animal and plant life, psychic transitions, atomic, cosmic, and evolutionary transitions, conspicuous transitions in nature (the transition of water into steam), etc. All of these examples offer another view of becoming, which, as we stated earlier also pertains to all such occurrences.

There is, however, also a difficulty that we met in explaining pure becoming. While it may not be too difficult to conceive transitions occurring in the just mentioned instances, it is very hard to think transition as such, in its purity. The reason for this is obvious. Both the human mind and language are glued, as it were, to the terms between which transitions occur, not to the processes of the transition going on between them. As it is well known, Aristotle connected the concept of "substance" with the noun in a sentence. Theoretically, a language that would not be oriented by terms of transitions, but by the transition only, would be purely verbal and consisting of only progressive forms without having nouns. Such a language is thinkable, and so is its mirroring the world as nothing but a world of transitions and of the being of transitions, rather than the being of entities. But humans do not have this kind of mind or language. They tend to the terms of transitions that are, however, "only" in between the terms. The terms are always in the foreground, their transitions appear to be of little practical importance.

But transitions do not only exist between two or more than two terms. There are transitions that we experience which have only one term; these are comparable to a relation having paradoxically one term. For example, I may meet a person who reminds me of someone else, whom I cannot identify, no matter how much I try to think and search. The face and look of the person I met is clearly given; on the other hand, the person he reminds me of is not. In a certain sense, one makes a comparision here to something that is not present at all. There are even relational experiences without terms, as we can have them in pure mathematics or in phenomenology. It may be that Heraclitus conceived Logos in this fashion: as becoming Be-ing without terms, or as pure transition that "collects" (legein: to collect) opposing terms.

Having partially explained the nature of absolute time up to this point, it has become more and more apparent that the nature of transitions, i.e., transition as an aspect of absolute time, cannot be explained with the aid of the concept of "relation" to be found among Aristotelian and Kantian, objective and subjective "categories." This can easily be seen when transition in absolute time is applied to two other Aristotelian or Kantian categories, viz. to potency and act, or respectively, possibility and actuality. Let us briefly do so in regard to Aristotle.

Aristotle clearly saw the connections existing between potency and act, on the one hand, and matter and form, on the other. Matter cannot be without form, i.e., it cannot be without being a particular kind of material. This is akin to saying that matter cannot be without form in the sense of shape. Form, therefore, actualizes matter. Without such actualization, matter remains a pure potentiality, or something that can only be logically thought, but does not exist. Figuratively speaking, and as is seen in Aristotle's system, our modern conceptions of chemical elements are "forms," or manifestations, of pure potentiality. Aristotle wants to say that potency can only be actualized by dint of form. Nevertheless, he also speaks of pure potentiality without form, viz. that which in Medieval thought was called the prima materia. Within the framework of his system, Aristotle is consistent enough to consider it a non-being, but non-being relative to being in-formal. In doing so, Aristotle leads us to think that potency is a realm "between" being and non-being, thus circumventing the pre-Socratic question of whether or not there is only being (Parmenides) or non-being (Gorgias). At least, the Aristotelian introduction of the notion of potency made it possible to leave behind the most difficult pre-Socratic questions of being, becoming, and nothingness (as impossible or possible to think): he conceived of the potency as nothing, but as relative to its actualization. During the Middle Ages, however, the materia prima had to be reinterpreted in light of creation. For everything had to be understood and believed to be as coming from creation. And with this, the ancient Greek stringency of thought that had potency where it logically belonged, i.e., as relative nothingness only, suffered dogmatic trimmings. The un-formed materia prima, too, was created now as "something."

Notwithstanding the long history of the changes of the concept of potency, creation, too, is transition and can only be thought of as such. It does not matter whether transition is said to be created or not. Creation cannot be conceived unless in terms of the transition of what is not to what is. In addition, creation implies that time, too, has been created, i.e., that creation did not occur "in" time, but is its own itself from nothing on the way to being. Transition does not, as we saw, necessarily mean that there must first be at least two given terms within which transitions take place; nor does it necessarily mean that there is one term turning into a transition toward another but still unknown and not given, as in a predictable childbirth. For birth to occur there must first be the mother and the transitions to the child born. Yet it can be said that there must first be a child for there to become a mother. The old paradox, which asks which comes first, the egg or the chicken, conviently supports the significance of the nature of transition, namely, that it is indifferent to the terms between which it occurs. Transition is in itself a form of being that continuously conceals itself behind our human tendency to look at its terms and things that are in transition, and the process of becoming rather than at transition and becoming itself in the relative absence of what is in transition or becoming. The being of transition is no thing. It is a pure temporal process. Aristotle's conception of time (the "whenever") as a category determining the substance, or as the form of how the substance appears, cannot be reconciled with the transition going on from potency to actualization. For Aristotle's conception of time is "of" something which moves and which is measurable in its motion. Time is the measure of the motion of "something" moving. Aristotle wants to say that, for example, the substance of a plant must be "sometime" and "somewhen," and its movement is determined by the measure of time. The substance "plant" has, of course, other accidental properties: it has "relations" to the soil and to the air, it has "quantity" and "qualities," etc. All nine categories that Aristotle established are active in determining substance, which is the tenth category of being.

By contrast, in the theory that I am developing, we have another picture: the transition itself going on from seed to plant, from potencies to actualizations, from relatively pure matter to form, and all actualization coming from the categories, possess the character of 1) self-activity and 2) of immeasurable temporalizations of every phase in the transitions. Indeed, on the basis of the above, one must come to the conclusion that if Aristotle had conceived of absolute time in our sense, all the transitions from matter to form, from potency to act, and in entelechy in general, he would have necessarily have been led to the assumption of absolute self-temporalization. Thus, his category "when" would not have turned out to be a property of substance, but a principle in Being itself, so that being and time would have appeared as "one" and the same and not as substance plus accident.

If it is the case, as we tried to show, that being is replete with transition in the sense as we believe Heraclitus must be read - the concept of time as form of self-activity cannot be separated from being at all. And this is the point where Scheler left off, and where we are beginning our task of continuing what appears to be a worthwhile thought.

In order to do justice to some of the very last thoughts of Max Scheler shortly before his death in 1928, we must comment on Heidegger's BEING AND TIME, which was published in 1927.

Up to this point, we set forth a number of practical examples in order to gradually bring absolute time into sharper focus. For this reason, our discussions remained in the realm of beings and entities, but did not touch on the question of Being itself. The question that comes up at his point is: Is there "one" absolute time over and above the various instances we have given of it? This is the question that Scheler raised in his essay "Idealism-Realism" after he had read BEING AND TIME.[5] In 1964, Heidegger told me that Scheler was occupied by the question of "temporality," "Dasein," and "death," as Heidegger clarified them in BEING AND TIME. In September 1927, Scheler wrote the aforementioned "Idealism-Realism," of which only parts two and three appeared during his lifetime. The fifth part was entitled "The Emotive Problem of Reality" and was exclusively concerned with Heidegger's work. Scheler died before completing the manuscript. This fragment was published in Volume 9 of Scheler's GASAMMELTE WERKE, along with all the marginals that Scheler made in his copy of BEING AND TIME, which Heidegger had sent to him immediately after it came out, and which I used for the edition of the marginals. The published fragment itself contains fifty pages that deal with "Dasein" in connection with anxiety and care. With respect to Heidegger's conception of temporality and death, nothing could be found among Scheler's papers.

What remains as a task, an important and difficult

one at that, is to see the connections between the temporality of Dasein and Scheler's understanding of it. Clearly, in the fifth part of "Idealism-Realism," he had the intention to tackle this problem.

We now conclude our explications of absolute time. In what follows, we must keep in mind three points: 1) the coincidence of meaning and phase, 2) the distinction between self-becoming and what comes-to-be in clock-time, and 3) transition. They must be thought together in one, no matter how difficult this may be.

PART II

THE IMPULSION OF LIFE

a) Ultimate Elements of Organic and Inorganic Energy

In determining the temporal components of the process of prediction-making, it was established that everything that has factually become in clock-time presupposes prior "becoming" of itself in absolute time; or, to put in other words, absolute time is pre-temporal in that it already elapsed prior to the objective clock-time "in" which something became real.

The term "prior," however, is only pertinent from the vantage poing of clock-time. As seen from the standpoint of clock-time, the self-becoming temporalization, it is true, looks as though it occurred before clock-time. But now we can also say that the term "prior" is not valid in the self-becoming itself. This is because the latter does not yet contain elements of clock-time at all. For this reason, it had to be argued that it is rather difficult to catch a glimpse of the very essence of self-becoming.

Any object of thought, including those of predictions, must nevertheless have relations with its own absolute becoming because the object of what is being predicted must be an object itself becoming in absolute time. The three aspects of absolute time (coincidence, self-becoming, and transition) served to clarify the nature of absolute time in general.

The experience of the nature of prediction, however, does not only require a clarification of absolute time. It does require, beyond any doubt, the clarification of two more items: a) a clarification of the nature of the mind through which predictions are made and b) a clarification of the general concept of life in which predictions are made.

Predictions are always made with respect to two objectives: 1) they are made with respect to what may or may not happen "in" human life itself, and 2) they are made with respect to what might or might not happen "for" or "onto" human life. A prophecy, for instance, essentially pertains to what will happen "in" human life, whereas weather forecasting, stockmarket projections, or scientific predictions of atomic radiation, or of earthquakes, pertain to what will or will not happen "to" human life. Predictions are either intrinsic or extrinsic to human life.

In what follows, we shall seek to clarify the concept of life insofar as it is necessary to do so for our goals. By itself, this concept requires much more of an investigation than has been done in the past. Aristotle was the first to give us a concept of life under the aspect of a grandiose conception, entelechy, i.e., the becoming actual of what is potential. The word "entelechy" comes from "en telei ekhein," which means "to be in perfection" or "to be in actuality." During the Middle Ages, the concept of life was understood in terms of the Holy Scripture, while at the beginning of modern times, especially with Descartes, the concept was narrowed to mechanistic scientific explanations (Lamettrie: "L'homme machine"), which remained predominant until the nineteenth century. It was only during the nineteenth century and during our own that the concept of life had been taken up again in purely philosophical studies, especially by Bergson, Nietzsche, Driesch, and Scheler. It was Scheler, however, who provided us with hitherto unknown studies of the interconnections holding between human life and mind. We will see in Chapter III what he came up with, restricting ourselves only to the essentials of his theories as they pertain to our objective of focusing on the foundations of prediction.

Within the very small scope of human perception, the distinction made between the organic and the inorganic world is as obvious as the distinction between space and time. They appear to us as separate aspects of nature. As far as space and time are concerned, however, Einstein showed that we can actually speak of "spacetime," i.e., as something which is one and the same. For Scheler, Einstein's findings touch upon the fundamental questions of physics, viz. those of the foundations of physics that he called "meta-physics." Those questions, he thought, had to be raised and organized in a future metaphysics.

But an analogous overcoming of the traditional distinctions made between organic and inorganic matter is not yet readily conceivable as the popularized unity of spacetime is in relativity physics. But Scheler thought this to be possible via "metaphysical probability."

Before we enter into the relevance this question has for our purposes, yet another question must be raised: isn't it true that, throughout the universe, there is an infinitely larger amount of inorganic matter than there is of organic life? Was the centrality of life in Nietzsche's philosophy out of proportion with this small, negligible planet called Earth, where there happens to be some life? Scientists have even begun to envisage a proof for the nonexistence of any life beyond the earth. Did we, too, as we must now ask, exaggerate the significance of self-becoming and absolute becoming in our previous discussion? For there is no doubt that the difference of the distribution of organic and inorganic matter in the world is in immense favor to the latter. The measure of life is infinitesimally small over against the inanimate, inorganic cosmos.

But there is also an unquestionable counter-argument against a Nietzschean or any other magnification of the role of life. It is the argument coming from the genius of Pascal, proclaiming that "Thought constitutes the greatness of man" and "By space the universe encompasses and swallows me up like an atom; by thought I comprehend the world." In Pascal's sketches of man, we are but a "reed" that is so feeble that the universe could crush us without any effort. But as a "thinking" reed, man is more noble than the whole universe. For the universe knows nothing of all this, only man does, via his mind

(PENSEES 346 ff.). The distribution of matter, life, and mind in the world has been assessed by philosophers in many ways. This question has its historical root in the pre-Socratic thinker Protagoras, who spoke of man as the "measure" of all. Clearly, the long history of the question deserves a separate study.

In the following, we follow the Pascalian view, rooted in Protagoras, by saying man is small, but that he is of the greatest measure over against the universe because he knows of all this. For the reaches of the mind extend far beyond the physcial universe. And since every act of the human mind, too, is of absolute time as we shall see, the question of absolute time is by no means dwarfed by the immensity of the distribution of inorganic matter. Indeed, the following will attempt to elucidate that the very opposite appears to be true.

In comparison to the vast scale of wave lengths that physics provides us, the visual spectrum of the scope of human perception, as that of any animal, is extremely small. But it was within this small scope that the stage for the understanding of nature had been set for a long time. Causality or cause-effect patterns were, for the most part, thought to be indispensible for the understanding of the world around us. We still use them in everyday predictions. It was only with the breakdown of classical mechanics in 1900, and with the discovery in the same year of Quantum Mechanics, that causality and other conceptions like "identity" had to be abandoned or considered anachronistic terms. The limited scope of human perception also suggests that inanimate matter (rocks, for instance) is something fixed and finished, while growing and dying life suggests something that will be forever unfinished. Thus, it was only a small step from these views to assume that inanimate materials precisely are what the term means, i.e., matter without biological life.

But in our century, the distinction between inanimate matter and living organisms has become blurred. The law of causality proved itself to be applicable and useful only within the small scope of perception: it failed in the subworld of the atom. Indeed, the entire range of atomic field-forces became subject to only one provable form of understanding: statistical laws. In addition, the traditional conception of "measurement" lost its universal applicability in the atom: measuring the temporal "impulse" of an electron implies the concomitant loss of the same electron's spatial whereabouts (Heisenberg), and vice versa. We know that it remains forever "uncertain" whether an electron "now" is the same as one observed "later." Hence, the old majestic law of identity, on which so much logic was dependent in the history of philosophy, lost its universal validity in the atom.

Both the small scope of human perception and the supposed universal causalities in nature have been explained in well-chosen examples. An hourglass filled with white and black sand will show the color gray, no matter how long the glass is turned. The chances that the black sand will be in the upper half and the white sand in the lower half are in practice nil. Cause-effect determinations apparent to our perceptions are comparable only to the statistical limits of the gray sand. This, however, does not make up reality.

In a similar fashion, and by way of example, Euclidean geometry was shown to be only a borderline case of non-Euclidean geometry prevailing throughout the universe (Riemann). It compares only to an infinitely small area of a huge sphere, and in which the area of the sphere's curvature is, in practice, nil. Euclidean geometry fails, of course, in large spatial dimensions, no matter how stringent it is in the infinitesimally small scope of human perception. Hence, during the first quarter of our century, a number of philosophical concepts, such as causality and identity, had to be redressed so that at least some commensurability with science could be retained.

This pertained especially to non-Euclidean geometry, which was first noted by Sacceri in Italy during the eighteenth century. This conception of geometry touched upon key notions in Kant's CRITIQUE OF PURE REASON, because Kant presupposed Euclidean geometry as well as causality in his entire work. Nevertheless, I wish to point to the very fact that Kant, too, must have caught a glimpse of non-Euclidean geometry when he maintained in the Critique that there was no contradiction in saying that two straight lines may inclose a figure (Figur)[1] and that three lines are not necessary. But one can also criticize Kant by saying that three perceived sounds should, on his premises, form a triangle, which, of course, they don't. Colors also should have been mentioned in Kant's table of categories, so one could argue. Overall, scientific and philosophical critiques of Kant as we find them in Scheler and others aimed at the "Euclidicity" of human perception that Kant had assumed. And in practical perception, Euclid's axioms are hard to verify. Standing between parallel railroad tracks, one "sees" them meet in the horizon, which, in fact, they do not. Perception resembles non-Euclidean geometry. The latter points, made by among others, Scheler himself, were only some of the many conjectures made concerning our perception as it is conjoined with the lived body and its schema. This configurement required completely new conceptions than were traditionally assigned to it. Early in this century, both Husserl and Scheler pointed to the significance to the "lived" body in its distinction to the body as an object. It is unfortunate that throughout the wide and intense research in this area, which later on were spurred on by Merleau-Ponty, one has not yet come up with a stringent topology of the lived body that could be acceptable to the sciences, especially the medical sciences. The tactile field of the lived body shows no Euclidean characteristics. Sensations of pain, for instance, can "migrate" and show a topology other than a Euclidean one, let alone a Cartesian, mechanical conception of the body could ever suggest.

We can now take up the aforementioned important question concerning the distinction between organic and inorganic matter. Scientific research suggested that the relationship between physical energy and vital forces had to be rethought. A mutation, it was suggested, had to be connected with a "quantum jump," implying that physics, dealing with inanimate matter, and biology, dealing with organic material, were actually not so far apart as they had hitherto been conceived to be. As early as 1926, Scheler forsaw this development of a rapprochement between physics and biology, and even a unification of them in terms of the foundations of both: in a "metaphysical probability" resting on pure insight and philosophical intution.

The tendency of interrelating the two sciences has been an area of intense research. Max Delbrück, one of its most representative thinkers and Nobel Prize winner in physiology and medicine in 1969, stated that the distinction between psychic and physical nature is not a radical one and that the distinction between external and internal reality is an illusion, stressing that in fact there is only one reality.

We cannot go into the details of Delbrück's theories, but in our context, we must at least mention his theory of the evolution of life.[2] He makes, in essence, two points: 1) life cannot have come from outer space to the earth, and because of the high exposure of cosmic rays, there cannot be life in outer space and 2) what did come from outer space, despite radiation, is only a "soup" from which organic molecules, such as H_2O, NH_3, CH_2O, etc., are easily formed. This "soup" possesses a striking similarity to Scheler's intuition of a universal, bioenergetic impulsion underlying both organic and inorganic material.

Organic molecules have an obvious similarity to atoms. Micro-organisms behave in terms of "stop-go" and "random walk" patterns, resulting from their random rotational diffusions and adaptation mechanisms. In addition, we find beginnings of perception in the micro-organic world.[3] But how can one verbalize the similarities between non-organic atoms and micro-organisms? In Delbruck's theory, there is a clear case for the transition from nonlife to life here on earth. And he conceived the explorations of how this happened as perhaps "the" fundamental question in biology. So did Scheler.

Scheler's intution and verbalization of this

transition, which must for us be conceived as happening in absolute time, runs as follows. The nonliving micro-material on which the existence of micro-organic matter is dependent, functions as a base for life. But it is organic material that is also gauged to, and engaged with, this base. In this engagement, there takes place what are called organic processes of self-temporalization, of becoming and un-becoming. While, on the one hand, atomic inorganic material constitutes extended field-forces, micro-organic material constitutes processes in time. But both inorganic field-forces and organic micro-centers of life obey statistical laws.

In this theory of the transition occurring between inorganic and organic micro-structures, the former functions as a catalysor, releasing micro-vital organization, which generates its own becoming and un-becoming in time, away from nonlife, if you will. While up to this point, Scheler's theory may be verifiable or not verifiable through scientific experimentation at some time in the future, the focal point of his theory, which is metaphysical, cannot. But it is all the more interesting. For he suggested that the cooperation of field-forces and micro-organic temporalization must presuppose a force that underlies both: a cosmic "impulsion" characterized by a four-dimensional expanse in which space and time are not yet distinct at all and of which nonlife and life are only two sides, one being the convex, the other the concave side of cosmic impulsion. Cosmic impulsion, therefore, is tantamount to a continuous creation of the world of field-forces and bio-centers alike, and it is well known that he assigned this aspect to the "becoming" unfinished Deity as one of its two attributes. Neither the philosophical nor the theogenetic implications concern us here. What is, however, of relevance to our subject is the possibility that cosmic impulsion itself is continuous becoming and that its own impulses of the smallest quanta bring about the effects of the maximum reality of the world. Of course, such impulses are metaphysical and, therefore, cannot be measured or verified; however, a metaphysical impulsion suggests the uncertainty of the location of an electron during measurement of its velocity, and vice versa, which is a shadow, if you like, of the very uncertainty in cosmic impulsion itself to posit in any of its smallest effects spatial field-forces or temporal life-centers. In any case, a pre-spatio-temporal becoming must be assigned to physical, inorganic material.

In the above, we have taken a wide detour around our subject, the nature of prediction. This was necessary for us to come to a sufficient, understanding of the nature of the mind and its relationship to life. Before we begin our discussion on the mind in the next chapter, we must take another look at life. We do this because the point can be made that the mind is gauged to, or engaged with, life just as this point was made earlier with regard to non-life and life. We shall leave our foregoing, more general discussion to examine some specifics concerning human life in particular.

b) Impulsion and Phantasy

In the above, we have always made an implicit distinction between two types of energy of life, or impulsion. Impulsion can be taken in a metaphysical, cosmic, or universal sense, and it can be taken in the sense that every individual organism possesses its own vital energy that keeps up and sustains all physical and biological functions, such as heartbeat, perception, circulation, feeling of body, etc. in the individual organism.[4]

Following the research that physiology provides us with today, it has also been shown that the first signs of perception can be found in micro-organisms, such as in bacteria, whereas the phenomenon of perception, it is implied, is not found in atomic field-forces. Perception, therefore, appears to be a unique phenomenon belonging to life only. The question that remains in philosophy of life is, however, how the origin of perception to be found already in rudimentary manifestations of life can, or must, be understood. What are the roots of perception, one may ask? Again, Max Scheler gives us a rather subtle answer to this question in his philosophy of perception, which was part of his essay on pragmatism ("Erkenntnis und Arbeit"). What, then, are the roots of perception?

In Section I b, "Becoming," we discussed the notion of vital motion vis à vis mechanical motion. It was stated that vital motion is characterized by having a "tendency" to move, which has its inception in its terminus a quo. That is, vital motion is, in contrast to mechanical motion, not determined by an endpoint, the terminus ad quem, much as vital motion, too, must have goals in its tendency of self-moving. But such goals are not determined by endpoints as those to be found in mechanical motion.

Vital self-motion must, in addition, have also "capacity to resist" and suffer all that it is exposed to from the outside. A cell delineates its own extension; in its becoming and un-becoming it spatializes itself. But doing so, it must "resist" all factors outside itself, including other cells, lest it loses its lived nature to grow and react. Strictly speaking, the non-living entities do not resist or react with or against each other in this sense. At best, they only interrelate according to the law of gravity. They have no center, sensation, or vital apparatus that could report lived resistance of outside factors. Hence, as seen from the inside of an nonliving entity, as it were, there is no world given to it, no reality. As Buddha once stated, it is extremely eerie "to be" a thing. In sharp contrast to this, a living entity has a lived relation to outside reality, which is given to it in its capacity to resist it.

The root of reality, therefore, is neither perception, nor consciousness, nor a category of reason, as Locke, Husserl, and Kant respectively argued. Reality is of a biological origin; it is rooted in the capacity of resistance that every organism has, beginning with the lowest and smallest micro-organisms. Perception takes its origin from resistance qua reality.

It is impossible, though, that what is "given in" the lived experience or capacity to resist would be devoid of any no matter how a vague whatness, i.e., without any significance given in an organic, resisting subject. Insofar as impulsion, i.e., the energy propelling the organism forward in every respect, is itself tendentious and "becoming" in its continuously supplying it with energy for all vital functions, impulsion, too, must have before it a vague kind of whatness toward which it relates. This is its phantasy. Every vital tendency goes toward something other than what it itself is. We find already in plants a slow "toward" light or "away from" darkness or in its roots a "toward" moisture and "away from" dryness. These phantasmic givens inherent in self-motion are called by Scheler "images" for want of any better term in a highly rational vocabulary in human languages. This image, given "in" vital reaction, including its basic impulsion, resembles the fabric of our dreams or swivelling outlines and colorations we experience while gradually waking up from narcosis in the absence of clock-time and of any awareness of our ego and person. It is not possible to describe these images sufficiently because our vocabulary is heavily oriented by our three-dimensional perception, not by our preconscious and pre-spatio-temporal experience of absolute time. It can even be maintained, as Scheler did, that nonlife entities, such as field-forces in physics, too, create their own proper images by dint of their own inherent self-motion sustained by the smallest effects of the impuluses in cosmic impulsion underlying both vital and force-centers. The wave-particle manifestation of the atom may well be such images, but as perceived or comprehended by man. For the images concerned must also have existence independent of the human observer.

The vague whatness, generated by and situated in all vital self-motion and its tendency, is rooted in reality qua resistance, i.e., in the capacity to resist what is outside, or different from, the resisting bio-center. Up to this point, the theory of impulsion and phantasy, stipulating that the vital energy or impulsion propelling all organic being and that all tendency of vital motion must have such images, owes us a clarification of how human drives have to be understood in such a context.

The answer is as follows: impulsion, endowed with phantasy, specifies in drives in organisms. Each major drive is tied to its own phantasmic images or drive-objects. Thus, the drive of propagation is tied up with the pure otherness in gender; the hunger-drive is tied up with unspecified food stuff, the power-drive with what might be called "more." Although all drive-objects are antagonistic to each other, they all drive forward into a pre-reflexive and preconscious vital "eagerness to learn and for something new." This vital curiosity situated near the center of life is, of course, not to be confused with the curiosity of an attitude of the mind. In addition, drive-objects are either central and "primary," or secondary, or "later." All instinctive behavior has the tendency toward the former pair. This can clearly be seen in the behavior of animals that select their foods in the wilderness or among birds building their nests out of material that is best fitted for its structure (drive of domestication). Because of this, drives are the first instances, no matter how vaguely, of the differentiation between space and time, and, therefore, what shows itself in space and time in perception. For what is central and signficant to a drive, or what addresses itself "first" in it, is "earlier," what does not, "later." Or, what is central to a drive is "nearer" in drive space, what is not remains in its background (even in factual perception based on this). Perception appears to allow mostly only such objects to fall into it that are central to drives; those objects are prone to be taken notice of earlier than what does not address a drive. A lizard's drive of self-protection makes it react instantly to threatening noises in the grass. But it remains put and undisturbed if one shoots a bullet from a shotgun. Its perception is delimited to this, but gauged to all the noises in the grass all the time. One can say that drives are glued to their objects, engendering respective types of behavior among the species.

The above mentioned eagerness to learn, inherent in drives, yields in man three types of knowledge. In higher animals, i.e., primates and men, this eagerness flows into "practical intelligence," which is the source of all pragmatic activity among higher animals and men that tends to get into control of objects by using them or trying them out (chimpanzee using stick). Science and technology have their source in the practical intelligence generated in the learning tendencies of drives.

Furthermore, the vital, preconscious desire to learn extends into the search for "salvage" of the herd or the group and functions here as the foundation of man's relatedness to the supernatural in myth. Gods, demons, and natural powers are experiences presupposed as real and are not questioned. All primitive religion rests in the drive for salvaging the life-communal group, such as family, clan, tribe, people. The loss of the mythic age and eras gives way to natural and positive theology in which religious objects become objects of rational investigation.

Finally, the drive-curiosity prying into the drive-objects develops into "astonishment" about what is new or about there being something rather than nothing. In man, this eagerness leads to knowledge of essence, or philosophy, and is perhaps indicative of an inborn drive in man to look "behind" reality in search of ultimate principles. Hence, the preconscious curiosity and eagerness to learn in drives is the source of the three kinds of knowledge in man: scientific knowledge aimed at controlling things in nature, knowledge of salvation or religion, and knowledge of essences, philosophy.

Two of the main human drives can easily be identified with two types of knowledge mentioned. The power-drive can be regarded as the source of all scientific, technical knowledge of control; the drive of procreation can be seen as the source of the tendency to preserve the herd, the group, family, clan, etc. But it is difficult to envisage the third drive of nutrition as being a source of, or even associated with, knowledge of essences and philosophy. Yet, Scheler seems to think so. He gives us some clues and perhaps convincing reasons that, at least in part, this connection holds.

At this point, we are in a new position to resume our subject of prediction, i.e., after having discussed some aspects of drive life, which, I propose, must not be ignored in determining the nature of prediction. For predictions are not infrequently motivated by human hopes, by deeply seated feelings of religious beliefs, or by our individual "feel" of being in this world or another past or future one. At least, this pertains to the frequently emotionally charged younger generations, which tend to project their own future, as we mentioned at the beginning of our investigation, according to what they believe is in their young power and often flamboyant anticipation.

According to the theory of impulsion and phantasy before us - taking into account the fabric of the three main human drives that to certain degrees must underly both thought and historical development - humanity has been, and is, passing through three different periods since man's first appearance on earth. These three periods reveal at least indirect influences of the three main drives. The first period is that of prehistorical and ancient times, in which man had to protect his group from outside intruders or attackers. In this period, the purity and preservation of the blood of the tribe was a primary value. The vital value series of honor, pride, courage, strength, esteem of family relations and ancestors, and the spirit of adventure and conquest were predominant values. Needless to say, that these values tied in with the drive of procreation insofar as this drive is felt to be in service of all social preservation and traditions. All Fascism is a futile attempt to renew these values, especially those of the so-called purity of blood (having nothing to do with the above), as well as the age of myth as an era also that is replete with brutal forces, where war and killing belong to life-values, i.e., the human tendency of gaining power over other human beings appearing that posed a threat.

As man began to become aware of history, the drive of procreation began to lose its subconscious, primary role in favor of the drive of power. The new predominance of this drive reaches as far as our own time and implies instinctive tendencies of gaining powers over other humans and over things in nature (the inception of technology). This second period climaxed in the global power struggles of the past and are still going on in our time, consisting of struggles between the superpowers and countless other conflicts between smaller nations, disadvantaged races and peoples that seek the same international power and recognition as predominant national or racial powers have.

But the third period of universal, human development, leavened by the drives, is said to lie in a predictable future, because there are unmistakable signs of its inception in our present. This future age, which Scheler calls "The World Era of Adjustment," rests on the predominance of a third main drive, the drive of nutrition. This drive motivates the mind to tend to gaining and increasing power over things alone, not over human beings, as is the case with the other two drives.

In short, the slow but steady decline of the predominance of the drive of procreation (coupled with an attitude of mind seeking dominance over others) and the subsequent slow but steady decline of the predominance of the power drive (coupled with continued desires to subdue others, but also with the desire of increasing controls over things in nature) is, over the vast ages, concomitant with a slow but steady rise of the predominance of the drive of nutrition coupled solely with an attitude of mind that seeks control and manageability over things only.

The mental attitude generated at least in part by the preconscious dominance of the nutritive drive can be called "to the things themselves," i.e., this drive has increasingly generated the age of economy for which the world is a composite of things to be controlled and used, managed, and marketed. A most obvious signal for the advent of this age is the fast rise of technology, gauged to the mastery of nature with its potentials and energies. In the future era, peoples will begin to set their quarrels aside and adjust to each other through communication, international exchange, etc. in a concerted effort to control and distribute the flux of things, goods, energies, and wares. The future, according to this theory, will be characterized by pragmatic circumspection and concerns; that is, mankind will be more busy with its global household. This preoccupation doing justice to the original Greek meaning of the word Eco-Nomy, House-Hold, will entail less war and pugnacious attitudes and thus it will be "less historical" because there will be less drama.

Indubitably, one can object to such a prediction on the grounds that our world today does not seem to be headed in that direction. On the contrary, the potential danger of war and annihilation of the human race is present everyday. Two world wars have occurred this century. A third one could happen at any moment. But one must realize that this theory is projecting very long ranges of historical periods, beginning with the first signs of human beingness on earth up until today. In this aspect, it more resembles a prophecy than a prediction; however, one can undoubtedly see signs today, even among superpowers and the like, that war begins to have a connotation of not being worthwhile. There are no winners, militarily or morally. At the base of this more prophetic theory of the effectiveness of the shifts among the three main drives and their dominance, going in the direction from procreation, to power and nutrition, war is merely "no good business." It is not eco-nomical for anyone.

Within a context proper to this study, however, the theory implies something more important. It is the only theory of historical projection that recognizes the significance of the importance of the distinction we made between what "comes-to-be," on the one hand, and pure "becoming," on the other. For we can now see that the shifts taking place among the three drives and their respective preponderance must have taken place in absolute time, whereas what we earlier called the "periods" of vast stretches of human history are the "shadows" in clock- or calendar-time with which the historian must work. The theory shows that history, past, present, and future, is anchored in the character of transition of absolute time among humans being in social contact with their respective epochs and phases.

We have stressed the possible functions of drives nourished by the vital energy of basic impulsion and its phantasy, being utilized in the images of drives and factual perception, because it may well be that the bulk of historical theories have taken too little consideration of their roles in human lives, individual or collective, in human actions, decisions, projections.

c) The Factors of Reality and Ideality

If reality, or what one calls "real," is not the result of visual or other perception, or of the result of activities of the mind, but is solely constituted by the factor of resistance implicit in any process of self-growth, then there must be factors in human life that are themselves the result of the self-growth, self-activity, and self-manifestation of the basic phenomena of self-becoming, impulsion, and drives. Drives show historical manifestation in "real factors." This is especially true with the three major drives we discussed, procreation- ,power-, and nutritive drives. Particular manifestations of such drives are called real factors, as opposed to "ideal factors," which are of mental origins.

Examples of real factors are: the distributions of populations, distributions among races, settlements conditioned by the structure of the earth's surface (geographic factors), geo-political distributions of power, power struggles including class struggles, competition, etc.; furthermore, economic relations and development among peoples and groups that often have global implications. These and other factors possess their own indigenous causations, similar to drives whose intensity, variablity, frequencies of welling up, and primary or secondary function in our practical lives are never under the complete control of the mind.

According to the theory before us, which stipulates that all reality and time is constituted in impulsive "becoming," there cannot be something like a "mind by itself" because it is the unlocalizable life-energy that is the presupposition for the mind's existence and activity. Mind, therefore, exists only "in function" with life and its energetic processes. Without life and impulsion, mind hangs in the air, unrealized. But this theory of reality also implies that there is no "one" universal mind. Mind can only exist in different groups. There are only group-minds or minds being in function with smaller or larger communities, or also civilizations. Mind occurs only in the embodied individuals. There is no mind detached from life. We shall take up this point in Chapter III.

Concerning the aforementioned real factors, one can say that they have turned into a mountain of problems today that are handled in terms of interdisciplinary considerations and studies. There are indications that they gradually will lose their own automatic positions within the scope of all real sciences. Indications are, for example, the increasing inseparability of domestic and foreign policy, of the problems and populations and work, and of economics and power politics. It is true that modern process engineering was able to make progress in understanding these overlappings and the distinctions to be made among real factors. But these findings rest most often on "models," or on formulas and formats, as we find them in cybernetics, information studies, or in public opinion polling.

In general, the explanations of interconnections among real factors, be they made in so-called interdisciplinary studies or process engineering, are highly abstract and, therefore, not infrequently fail to prove themselves in the concrete, given situation. The common and subtle skepticism of the everyday individual reflects this, viz. that when the common man is every so often dished out the boring prediction - especially after an election or prior to the beginning of a five-year economic plan in socialist countries - that the economy might turn worse before it will get better. A real factor, such as the economy, can only be partially comprehended in terms of logical or discursive thinking and abstract models. This is because economic development has its ultimate foundation in drives. Its development is rooted in absolute becoming; logical models, or the like, just do not fit. An economic prognosis may be made for a period of six to nine months, as is the case, for instance, with a "J curve," projecting the delay of the effect of a lower or devalued dollar has with respect to more export. As we all know, the expectations concerned in this often remain far from being fulfilled. According to our components of prediction thus far established, the lowering of the dollar in fall 1986 will not result in higher exports hoped for. Why? First of all, such prognoses utilize clock-time and conceive of the future in abstract terms. The future is a box "into" which forecasts are made or taken out, as the expression goes. Hence, they are oriented around what "comes-to-be," and not in terms of economic "becoming." While abstract prognoses are continuously being made, the indigenous development of the real factor of economy itself has already run ahead of model-making and abstract constructions. That is, the becoming of economic factors is ahead of the model of what is supposed to come to be.

We find here an interesting aspect of prediction-making. The relative slowness of the effect that drives have throughout history mentioned earlier ("drive shifts") has suddenly disappeared for us in the above example in favor of a very rapid effect that drives have or can have in historical processes. But this does not say that there will be a quicker or better prognosis. In the above example, the negative effect that the lower dollar has on foreign imports, for instance, is not covered by the J curve; nor can the J curve cover it. The prognosis concerned is at best true if it touches upon the threshold of the self-becoming of economic tendencies in those foreign countries, and it lies not in the decision to devalue the dollar. The affected foreign economic tendencies that escape such prognosis cannot be fully expressed in models, graphs, or strategies.

The deficiency in predictive models pertains to all behavior of real factors. It can even be seen in such predictions, which upon first sight, have very little to do with real factors such as weather forecasting. The indispensible scientific method of simulation is also used in meteorology. A three-dimensional lattice covering a simulated globe shows the various weather-forces working at the thousands of lattice intersections and describes the behavior of weather patterns in the very near future in terms of differential equations. From this, forecasts can be made. The tighter the lattice, the better the prediction. But there is a limit. If the lattice is, say, cut in half, implying eight times more intersections, the time-factor, too, must be reduced, necessitating an increase of the computation speed-up to more than the tenth power so that the prediction could be made in time. Even the capacity of machinery like the Cyber 205 cannot handle this. The weather-forces are ahead of it all. Even in such geographic and meteorological cases, then, our philosophical distinction made between coming-to-be and becoming holds, or, put in other terms, the distinction between clock-time and absolute time. It would appear that we can have knowledge of the real factors only in terms of what they have just been or how they just showed themselves to us. But we seem to be unable to determine them in their a quo tendencies, should we continue to try to grasp them only in terms of logical or statistical models.

This state of affairs, it must be added, is quite compatible with the nature of historical facts, because historical facts are open in themselves and, for this reason, neither fully predictable nor controllable. If there were a possibility of exact predictions made through technical models, one could expect them to be possible only by means of a "logic without reasons," i.e., a logic devoid of quantitative and discursive concepts, but equipped instead with exclusively topological-morphological factors. This would enable us to leave behind our traditional projections in terms of what "comes-to-be" in favor of reaching the borders of a quite different predictability of what is "becoming." We do not know today whether such a logic, which is not logic in the traditional sense, exists or can be constructed.

Today, a similar situation exists in computer technology, the principles of which rest on two-dimensional space. Even if we could construct a three-dimensional computer, it would still be insufficient to capture the four-dimensional expanse of impulsion, which, as a unity of drives, is the foundation of all real factors.

On the basis of the above, one can argue with justification that the technical knowledge of what may come to be at the expense of a philosophical insight into the becoming of real factors represents the elbow-room of the unreliability of technical prediction. For in it, we deal with the future as though it were a thing that has to be worked on; but we forget that this thing itself is becoming in absolute time. In doing so, we jump over thousands of forms of chance happenings that befall us throughout our lives and history itself. Even more, in light of our distinction between what comes-to-be and pure becoming, technical models, which serve the predictability of whatever states of affairs they are offered to, begin to resemble molds that technical man tries to impress upon the flux of life and its real factors. While such models can be of great service at times, they remain, because of their static character, inadequate in catching the undercurrents of transitions concerning real factors in life.

Our attempt to clarify the concept of life with respect to prediction leads us necessarily to our next focal point of the discussion: the very origin of prediction-making, the human mind. For in all of the above, including our digressions, we always presupposed the functions of the mind in understanding what had been said. We must ask whether the mind, too, is of a "becoming" nature and whether all decision-making, whether "true" or "false," "good" or "bad," "good" or "evil," "appropriate" or "inappropriate," presupposes absolute time. In order for us to be able to catch a glimpse into the nature of the mind with respect to predictibilities, it was necessary to look at "becoming" from as many angles as possible.

In what follows, "becoming" will reveal itself from entirely different aspects, which, I believe, have not been given due consideration yet in analyses of the nature of the human mind. We shall ask the question how mental insight, ideas, or intuitions, relate to what is real and existing. What is the relationship of evidential knowledge to real factors, for instance, to those of economy? How do we have to conceive the relationship that the mind has to beings or things? How does this relationship - if it can sufficiently be described and presented - appear to us in the context of prediction?

PART III

MIND AND THE GENESIS OF HUMAN IDEAS

a) Two Examples for the Genesis of Ideas in Greek Philosophy

The Greeks were the first to develop theories concerning an answer to the question of how human ideas come about and how their origin must be understood. We bring into focus two such theories in order to juxtapose them in this section with a third, more recent position concerning this question. The third position is not only the one developed by Max Scheler, but in essence also concerns a prevalent and original philosophical outlook: pragmatism.

The first ancient theory was developed by Plato. It holds the following: if a human being looks at two equal things, say, two equal tents, the idea (eidos) of "equalness" must be pregiven in his perception. This is because they are tents and not "equalness." The idea of equalness cannot be in the tents. It must be of another kind of being that is distinct from the visible, existing tents. The idea of equalness, therefore, is a possession (of the soul) of the human being; it cannot have its origin in the tents or any other things that are equal in our perception. Hence, the idea of equalness, as any other idea of this type, is inborn. For in order to be able to perceive the two tents as "equal," one must already have some knowledge of what "equalness" means or is. That is to say, we must be in possession of this idea prior to the two tents.

The second ancient theory we will explicate asserts the contrary. It goes back to Plato's student, Aristotle. But Aristotle did not present his theory as is often said he did. Therefore, we refer to this second theory as the pseudo-Aristotelian theory, keeping in mind that when one takes a close look at the original texts of Aristotle - something we cannot do here - Aristotle's theory is not all that contrary to Plato's as it may look at first sight.

The pseudo-Aristotelian theory asserts that the idea of equalness presupposes the perception of the tents. We must first see the tents, and only then can we have knowledge of the equalness of the two tents. In a way, the idea is here drawn out of the seen tents, or, as it is said, the idea is "abstracted." Hence, the idea of equalness is an abstraction of the mind. The initial point of the genesis of the abstraction is the sensory datum of the entity in perception, in our case, two tents. Hence, perception is the presupposition of an idea.

These two theories, which stipulate that an idea must either be inborn or be the result of abstraction from sense experience, have, over the centuries, each found different arguments of support. In our days, it can be held that scholars of pure mathematics, i.e., not of applied mathematics, almost unanimously agree that Plato's argument is closer to the truth. For they justifiably can say that if it were the case that numbers - which are neither things nor tents- were abstracted from things, it could never be the case that irrational numbers or infinities or powers (Cantor), or the number zero for that matter could be abstracted from a thing. In sharp contrast to such a position, however, are, among other disciplines, the social and political sciences as well as economics. They tend to follow, albeit mostly without cognizance, in all of their activities the Aristotelian line of thinking by giving preference to sense data over against ideas and conceptions. As it is the case among present-day politicians also, the social scientists speak a great deal of theory and practice, stressing the indispensable role practice has in our lives, and with respect to our example, the practice in handling or dealing with tents. For it is important that tents are marketable, or that they point to the general animal tendency to find shelter with its simultaneous social contact. To a theory that stresses "practice," equalness appears to be at best an uncomfortable X not contributing much to social life, and the idea of equalness has the air of something strange, esoteric, or even funny about it, notwithstanding the fact that social scientists speak about equality, say, among humans. Computer science, too, presupposes the pseudo-Aristotelian theory. The computer is fed with data given in experience. Only then does it serve its function to calculate, order, prognosticate, or give indications from such data or transform them into graphs, etc. Our age of technology is thoroughly un-Platonic. Modern man is glued, as it were, to sensory data. The meaning or sense of what is nonsensory, as the idea of equalness, or say, the meaning or sense of the Divine in a nonsensory experience of humility, does not seem to be so topical it has been in former ages.

The theories of the genesis of ideas in Plato and in Aristotle are basically incompatible. Equalness is either in us or it presupposes things in perception, which, subsequently, are looked at as being equal.

It is not the business of philosophy to opt for one or the other theory. If it were, philosophy would be tantamount to having standpoints, that is, philosophy as a whole throughout history would have to be considered as nothing but an conglomeration of various standpoints, even contradictory ones at that. Standpoint-philosophy has increased along with the increase of the disciplines in both sciences and the arts. All too often in the past two centuries, philosophy has consisted in part of "schools." But as history shows us, since the decline of Greek philosophy when schools were so popular, philosophical schools have always been short-lived. The Marburg School and the Frankfurt School are only two out of many examples in our own time.

Schools of philosophy and standpoint-philosophy in general, contradict the essence and intention of philosophy. None of the twenty or so great philosophers who lived since Greek thought meant to found a "school" or promote a standpoint. Standpoints in philosophy seem to have two conditions on which they thrive: 1) they come up when a specific philosopher is discovered posthumously, and is researched intensely to the effect that he generates disciples and 2) they come up when persons dealing with philosophy skillfully promote their standpoints such that a school will ensue. In this case, philosophy resembles a business that is run by effective people. The first condition for standpoint-philosophy was generated, for instance, by neo-Kantians, Platonists, and Aristotelians. The second condition was generated by many people, even in our time. Courtesy forbids names to be mentioned. But we do not want to imply that in both cases, above all in the first, knowledge of essence has been gained, indeed, often very valuable knowledge. Where would philosophy be today without the great Aristotelians of the Middle Ages?

In our context, the essence of philosophy comes to the fore for us in terms of the very insight into the contrariness itself of the above two ancient theories. The essence of philosophy does not come to the fore for us in terms of an option between the two. For philosophy is knowledge and cognition of the nature and essence of objects. And the nature and essence of equalness, for example, cannot be defined in either of the two theories. This essence remains concealed in philosophical knowledge and cognition itself. For this reason, philosophical cognition is always connected with concealing. In this regard, Scheler said one time that any theory of knowledge and cognition presupposes knowledge and cognition of itself. Theory of knowledge is possible through knowledge only. It implies a circular activity.

Philosophical thought must not merely follow theories, as the Platonic or Aristotelian one concerning the genesis of ideas making up human knowledge, and, consequently, the structure of our lives. While philosophy must always be aware of such theories, it must at the same time have the purpose of rethinking such theories ever anew and to think through all aspects that surround a theory. This includes philosophical standpoints. Whenever philosophers think "around" the essence of an object and try to get behind its surface to penetrate into the core of meaning, they meet with something that most often remains incomprehensible to the everyday understanding. For this reason, many great philosophers were not recognized in their own days. The Greek word for "around" is para. The Greek word for standpoint or opinion is doxa. Philosophical paradoxes often defy common sense in their logicality and stringency and, in doing so, enhance and provoke the Socratic courage to think around standpoints so that the essence of an object comes to the fore, regardless of standpoint or common understanding.

As long as man has lived on this planet, the incomprehensibility of Being has always challenged and fascinated him. This equally pertains to the Chines Tao, the Asian Indian Nirwana, to the Greek Alethia, as well to as the Deity, no matter in which paradoxic terms these showed themselves in man's thought. We have every reason to believe that in the future, too, man will be addressed by the incomprehensibility of Being. This incomprehensibility does not stem from man's inability to think. On the contrary, man is always already given to Being and its Presence before him. But this presence is "given" to him only in pure thought, not in terms of ordinary opinion or discursive thinking. Later on, we enlarge this point.

b) Contemporary Conception of Ideas: The Essence of Pragmatism

It was only recently that a new alternative had been found to the two Greek conceptualizations of the nature of a human idea and its genesis. This alternative has penetrated almost all research in whatever field and discipline of knowledge, but not often has it been recognized as a genuine philosophical insight. Its source is American pragmatism. Pragmatism does not concentrate so much on the nature of the ideas as the Greeks did; nor does it concentrate so much on the nature of things as the Greeks also did. Rather, pragmatism focuses on human actions, which, no doubt, are conjoined with both the nature of ideas and the nature of things. But this concentration on the nature of human action was not a deliberate effort to find an alternative solution to Plato and Aristotle. Rather, the focusing on action is an autonomous theme by itself in the philosophy generated by Peirce and James.

It is unfortunate that up until now European philosophers, educators, politicians, and researchers of rank have, with the exception of Max Scheler, not seen the importance pragmatism plays in our time. In the standard works of European philosphers of our century, pragmatism is mentioned only peripherally, if at all; and when it is mentioned, it is in depreciating context. The fact of not taking seriously standard texts in pragmatism may have something to do with anti-American tides that swept off and on in Europe since World War II. Today, European leftist jargon refers to everything American as naive or decadent; the same jargon, by the way, was used during World War II by the Fascists. Even some European textbooks used in high schools show an anti-American twist.

The fact that pragmatism had its origin in America, however, or the fact that idealism and realism had their origins in Greece, the Tao in China, the Nirwana in Asian India, is uninteresting and not pertinent to philosophy. Philosophy is no cultural geography. We fully support in this respect Scheler's contention that European philosophy must still have a lot to learn from China and India and that it had exaggerated its philosophical role in the past. There is a lot to be learned from pragmatism also, and, although Scheler does not seem to have made a note of it, his own work on pragmatism strongly suggests that it was meant to be read by the European intellectual for at least a preliminary orientation. Throughout his entire philosophical activity, Scheler occuptied himself with pragmatism.

What is pragmatism's message and what are its guiding principles?

Pragmatism takes into focus the function of actions and truth. Something is true only when it proves itself in action (Greek: to pragma, action, execution). What, however, does "to prove itself" mean? It means that something proves truth in action and in acts, and that this being-true preserves itself through such an action and act.

What does the term "true" mean here? Is it not the case 2x2=4 is true even without an action? Other questions press for answers in this context. What is the relationship between truth and insight? Is it not the case that the cognition that 2x2=4 is an unquestionable insight, but also 2x2=5 is an insight into what is false? If so, human insight is indifferent to truth and falsity. Indeed, insight is the domain within which the true and falsity come to be distinct. Insight is seeing that something is true or false, but insight itself is not "true" as an opposite to false.

Such arguments concerning insights, or what is more often refered to as "judgements," have been known since Greek philosophy and are basic to modern logic. Yet, both symbolic logic and the above propositions concerning insight, true and false, presuppose that insight belongs to the domain of judgement. Judgements are the domain of logical stringency. But this is not the case with insight. For this domain, too, can be made an object of insight. Judgement is not insight. Insight always presupposes itself if we make judgements on it.

One can go on and on in asking such questions. But the nature of insight will not be grasped in such questions. This is because it, too, is an insight to say that there is no insight into insights possible, or put in other terms, insight cannot see into itself. All seeing of opposites, like truth and falsity, presupposes an overview of insight into both, but there is no insight of insight. In a way, insight is blind to itself. It remains dark in its own nature. Insight resembles the seeing of the eye. The eye may see anything except itself. The eye is its own blind spot.

In the thinking of opposites, and not only of truth and falsity, philosophical thought has, since the pre-Socratics, been clearly distinct from everyday discursive thinking. It was especially Heraclitus, called "the dark one" (ho skoteinos), who thought into opposites, like day and night, life and death, etc. He thought them, paradoxically, to be one and the same. This is a most difficult thought and perhaps we cannot retrace its nature completely. But on the basis of the above, it is thinkable that opposites are "one" in terms of insight and overview and its indifference to opposite terms. It is thinking proper, as Heidegger calls it, and consists in letting lie before one the presence of all there is, including what is true and false. But this letting lie before one is not the result of our own decision or will. On the contrary, the letting lie before us in its presence is not the result of a subjective endeavor, but the presence of all is "always already" with us and has always already befallen us. We are enveloped in the very looking of the presence of Being, and it is only because of this that we are able to relate to entities in Being itself. Preconscious, ecstatic thought was also elaborated by Scheler in his work on THE NATURE OF SYMPATHY. We cannot deal here with this most important issue in contemporary philosophy. But we must mention it because prediction - whatever its nature and possibilities may be - also presupposes in any of its occurrences Being within which they are made, and through which they become possible to be made correctly or falsely.

Pragmatism thinks truth in conjunction "with" things and states of affairs in which this truth is supposed to prove itself. Truth reveals itself in and during actions and in dealing with things. In saying that truth proves itself with things and actions, it is denied that truth exists prior to or after the perception of things. Truth takes place and happens along with things that are being handled. It does not take place in a physical sense of "place"; rather, its taking place is purely temporal. Truth should not be taken in the sense of a noun; instead, truth is truth-being whereby being is to be taken in its progressive form of "to be": be-ing. In being temporal and occurring "with" things, truth-being is neither before things, ante res, as Plato's innate ideas prior to perception and nor after them, post res, as Aristotle's abstraction from and after perception suggested. In this sense, pragmatism is a most viable alternative to the age-old Platonic and Aristotelian arguments and perhaps a most important asset in the history of philosphy. Truth-being is cum rebus, an expression which James also once used, but which Scheler used rather often to make the point. The pragmatic cum rebus character of truth-being also underlies Heidegger's "at-handedness" in Being and Time.[1] For it is said here that things show themselves during their use and while being used. But Heidegger fails to see the pragmatic root of this in pragmatism, although he does use the term "pragmatic" in its original Greek meaning. Heidegger does not mention either that the meaning of things coming about while handling them must be of the temporal nature of "becoming," i.e., absolute time; nor does he seem to see the significance of the coincidence of meaning and phases running off while the thing is being handled. Of course, in his own context, these points may not have been so important as they are for us.

There is no doubt that Scheler was motivated by the pragmatic argument, much as his own descriptions may not always be completely in line with James. The pragmatic ways of explaining our knowledge of things and of truth-being were, however, so important to him that he thought our whole age, and its mentality, must be seen in connection with it.

Before clarifying the quintessence of pragmatic truth - the clarification of which, in our view, is indispensable to coming to grips with the nature of prediction - we must briefly explain the term "essence" as it is used in what follows. The ancient, crystally clear meaning of this and other terms such as "substance," "phenomenon," etc. have in our time been deprecated, at times beyond their recognition through everyday discourse and misuse of language. Before they are used in philosophy, they have to be properly clarified. The usage described here is commensurate with that of Scheler's phenomenonology, the details of which do not concern us here. Of course, other uses of such terms also exist in philosophy.

1. In the foregoing considerations, we used the term "image." Its general genesis was said to begin with all self-activity generated in what we called cosmic impulsion and its phantasy. Hence, there are both vital and atomic energetic centers, followed by those in plants, animals, and man. In man, this phantasy is commonly referred to as "imagination," which works itself up even to the most abstract intuitions in mathematics. The specific genesis of images correlated to every self-activity in man begins, it was said, in the individual's own impulsion-phantasy, followed by drive-images, images in perception, and again in the mind. The term "image" is in all of this equivalent with the term "basic phenomenon." Therefore, a basic phenomenon belongs to all self-activity, not only to man's.

2. In the previous considerations, we referred to human "ideas." This term is equivalent to "meaning." Ideas, of course, are of the order of the mind.

3. If an image of impulsion-phantasy, i.e., when a basic phenomenon and an idea are congruent with one another, we have a primordial "essence."

On this basis, we can now say: impulsion-images generate primordial "essence" whenever they are congruent with ideas, and vice versa. When this happens, the essence is situated at the thresholds of life and mind. That is, an essence lies in between the impulsion-image and an idea of the mind. "Essence" is their meeting point. Therefore, essence is neither image alone, nor an idea alone. Its occurrence lies in their congruent conjunction.

c) The Essence of Pragmatic Truth: Functionalization

As a result of the previous discussions, we supplied some definitions. These definitions enable us now to get a close look at the point of departure from which a prediction has to be made. It will be contended that if this point of departure is not taken into consideration, a prediction will inevitably go astray. That is, whenever a prediction misses the essence constituted by life and mind, it cannot come to be realized in practice, unless by rare chance. If a prediction does, however, hit or otherwise take into consideration the mind-life-essence, it is bound to have at least limited success. At this point, we must leave aside the question of the degree of difficulty that the latter must imply.

Another consideration concerning the nature of prediction offers itself at this point: all predictions are either spatial or temporal. They pertain to either more spatial aspects as those contained in all real factors, or they pertain to more temporal aspects as they do with regard to the historical mind.

Spatial predictions are, for example, weather forecasts. They are based on constellations of extended data such as lows, highs, flare-ups on the sun, geographical locations (coast, inland, etc.). Spatial predictions are, as a rule of thumb, more manageable than temporal ones because they can be graphed or charted so that we can "see" what the tendencies are or could be. But one should not exaggerate the success of this type of predictability. Despite the technology amenable to spatial predictions, the net value and success of them is rather disappointing as compared with their immense dollar-value investments. The behavior of insects, for instance, can be as foretelling and effective as computers and weather satellites - and so can an experienced farmer in his own location.

The temporal predictions are far more difficult and pertain to all that may or may not affect our own person and even the history of mankind. They do not allow of technological device as spatial predictions do. No technical device can predict what the world will be like tomorrow. It may be in shambles. At best we can make a good guess at it. Nor can any machine predict whether we ourselves or someone near us will suffer a stroke tomorrow, much as medical likelihood is given by statistical data in certain patients. Prophecies appear to be the most pure temporal form of prediction.

Strictly speaking, however, predictions are not so distinct in their spatial and temporal relevance. Both characters seem to occur in one and the same object and it is up to the type of prediction made which aspect, the spatial or temporal one, is presupposed or under consideration. Today, human beings tend to stress the spatial aspect of predictions because of the mass of machinery available to them on which they so heavily rely. But spatial aspects of predictions need not at all be dependable on machinery. I may plant a tree in my backyard, believing that it will provide some shade in particular areas during future hot summer days. This spatial prediction of shade cast at a future date in a certain area is rather dependable. But it is not easy to predict whether the tree will be there for the next generation or so for me to enjoy its shade. It might get sick and die. Its longevity is known only through statistical data concerning the average lifetime of this particular tree.

Research to be made in classifying predictions may at some time reveal that there are rather curious admixtures of their space and time components. A classic example is economics. Economics is, on the other hand, attached to spatial predictabilities such as the seasons, crops, weather, productivity, basic materials, availability of gold or platinum in geographical and geological locations, etc. But, by contrast, market tendencies are not localizable. They are at least of a partially temporal character, or at least to a high degree, as is indicated by the important factor of the "psychology" of a market, or by the psychic contagion that can sweep the floor of the stock market, God knows why, and let the market go wild in a bullish or bearish direction. When psychic contagion takes over, no common denominator can be found in any explanation of the turbulent market pursuant to the psychic market explosion.[2]

Having all the above in mind, we want to approach the nature of pragmatic truth, since it is this kind of truth that appears to "fit" prediction-making. Or did we just say "kind" of truth? There are, indeed, various kinds of truth to be found in the history of ideas and philosophy. Unfortunately, we are only rarely aware of them. Heidegger showed convincingly that truth has its own history, which, in turn, is based on the ancient Greek experience of truth as Un-Concealment, or "A-Letheia." Unconcealment or Aletheia is the unconditional Presence of what is, regardless whether something is true or false, good or bad, just or unjust, etc. In light of the history of truth, the pragmatic truth, too, appears to be only a variation, if not a deviation or even aberration, of the original experience of Unconcealment. The latter stems, so Heidegger showed, from the thought of Heraclitus, Parmenides, and Anaximander, as far as we know today. We will not deal with this important issue of the history of thought, which, so Heideggerians argue, casts essential light on our own times.

We will again use the method of exemplification in order to bring into focus our object of discussion: pragmatic truth. Let us look back at the two tents. Following our definitions of terms, the two tents must be perceived both in terms of their "images" generated by impulsion, which, in turn, fans them into drives, as well as by the "idea" of a tent. The idea of the tent is real only if it meets with the image in impulsion and drive-attention. If this does not happen, the idea of the tent remains unrealized. The same holds true for the equalness among the two tents discussed earlier.

What, however, is this "image" supposed to be? It is said to be that factor which realizes the idea of the tents and thereby proves the idea to be true. The image in impulsion, and its self-activity, is a "gestalt" given in phantasy. With what is the gestalt concerned? We can perceive a tent in various ways. We see the tent fluttering in the wind. We feel the tent while setting it up. We smell the tent, especially when it is new. We can taste the tent if our tongues happen to touch it, as in the case of inquisitive small children. All these experiences are segments of perception, which, taken all together, form the gestalt of the tent. According to our definition, they are rooted in drives with their own images, no matter how blurred they must be on their sub-conscious or pre-perceptive levels. But these drive-images, too, have segments of their own, forming drive-gestalten. In spotting a tent in perception, the drives of domestication of the group or herd, the drive of procreation, are at work playing their roles and functions. They are in the neighborhood of the drive of shelter and self-protection. Yet, without the idea of what a tent is, these images remain blind, and it is only in the presence of the idea of the tent that they function as a factor or realization. Both image and idea must be in function with each other for the tent to become what it is. Without the life of images coming from drives and their life-center, impulsion, the idea of the tent is not given, nor is its essence.

It is only by dint of the meaning "tent" that the images in drives become themselves something tentlike, and similarly, the idea of the tent is only given with the image. The essence, therefore, of something proving itself to be truly what it is lies in this case, in the interpenetration, i.e., the functionalization of the idea and impulsion-phantasy. In the given example, the phantasmic, preconscious image of "sheltering" realizes the idea of a tent. The realization of an idea is therefore a process in conjunction with impulsion and its self-moving activity. Impulsion and mind must, therefore, not be taken in a dualistic sense, but in a sense of functional interpenetration. A world without ideas is thinkable. It would consist of phantasmic images given in animals and also probably in plants. It was, indeed, a world prior to the advent of man.

Ideas, then, do not exist in an ideal realm. Without life and its factor of realizing impulsion, they have no existence of their own. Nor does the mind have existence of its own. The mind's existence is, as far as we can see and know, only with life. As we mentioned earlier, a pure mind, a pure consciousness, and a pure ego are, according to such a view, impossible constructions.

In order to bring into bold relief the concept of

the functionalization of ideas, a Schelerian analogy of the essence of the mind offers itself.[3] The analogy has, briefly stated, four steps and runs as follows:

1. Ideas of the mind and the mind itself are powerless, as is the symphony in the mind of the composer only. Unless the symphony, say Beethoven's Fourth, is performed and conducted it has no power to realize itself.

2. Beethoven's Fourth is dependent upon the performance of the conductor and the orchestra. In this analogy, the conductor has the function of impulsion or the life center, serving as a principle opposite the ideas of the mind. All musical images of the symphony remaining in Beethoven's mind only stay there. They require a life-center to become real. The existence of the images and ideas of the symphony is one of "continuous becoming" with conductor and orchestra. The ideas of the symphony are becoming and un-becoming in each phase of the performance, i.e., in the absolute time of pure listening to it. The analogy can also be extended into the area of light. If light does not hit a surface, its waves remain dark. Light realizes itself only with things and surfaces.

3. But neither the composer nor the conductor alone can account for the realization of the symphony. There must be the orchestra. In the analogy, its players stand for the various drives with their own particular images. On the one hand, they cannot play without a conductor who guides them. On the other, the conductor cannot do without them who play with him.

4. Finally, the instruments stand for all physical factors necessary for the audibility of the symphony, sound waves, air, even their atomic compositions. Without them, there is no symphony, either.

Hence, the ideas of the symphony are real only by way of their functinalization with their conductor (impulsion), orchestra (drives), and instruments (physical factors). In this analogy, ideas by themselves are not really extant. They are at best in potency to become realized sometime in the future.

This holds for mind also whenever its ideas do not find functions with things in life that bring them alive and make them historical. Overstating the argument, we could say: mind's ideas can exist only if they are conjoined with the blood of life.

Despite the negation of the mind's autonomous existence, we nevetheless have gained some insights into the mind. For it can only be in the form of absolute time that ideas and the mind can realize themselves with life. Both ideas and mind have the temporal form of "becoming," of "coincidence" and of "transition." Ideas become with impulsion; they coincide with phantasmic images and they are continuously in transition toward newer and newer images: they are functionalized realization.

This, however, necessitates a third factor of the process of the realization of an idea. For if the mind by itself does not exist, it must have a form of its manifesting itself while being in conjunction with the life-center. This manifestation of the mind is its personhood. Personhood is the form of the mind becoming in absolute time with life. Or, person is mind realized. There is no mind accessible to us unless it is in some form of person. No devil and no god is without personhood.

Naturally, there can be large differences of realizations of ideas among individuals and groups and, hence, among persons. But these differences must not only be explained in light of difference in character, differences of group-minds, and of zeitgeister in cultures. They must also be a result of differences in the constellation of drives and their images, of their prevailing or weak roles in the individual's or the group's life. The Asian Indian culture did not develop technologies, or the art of martial strategy, or a stock market only because its mind or spirit is different from that of the West. The reason is that its power drive was, and is, less proponderant among drives than it is in Western culture. Instead, it seems, its drive for shelter and salvation is much more distinct. It developed extremely sophisticated psychic techniques of overcoming suffering without external means as well as the typical Asian virtue of patience. Nature is not an object to be exploited and utilized. It is a part of the life of the individual who lives in and with nature. These and many more differences must also be accounted for by the more difficult grasp of drive-constellations, having their ups and downs collectively as they do in the individual. The preponderances and weaknesses, the activity of drives and their dormancy, resemble tides in their lives and manifestations, which, as we know, are also in tandem with the aging phases of the individual and, perhaps, of cultures.

A philosophy of prediction for which we are trying to give some outlines - not shrinking back from taking detours in the jungles of preconscious interests, images, and tendencies - must always take into account such tides and constellations in our drives because they do exert their often very hidden influences on the becoming of ideas of the moment and of future projections. A theory of prediction that does not do this remains a "u-topia," i.e., a theory that will find "no place," as the word "utopia" indicates, in the tides of practical life. It will remain a theory presupposing that human intelligence - even in its surmised duplication of "artifical intelligence" as it is called - alone is the essence of man, and that our drive-life, our emotions and feelings, and above all, our imagination are but inconvenient attachments to an intelligent, and ever obedient, impersonal robot-machine-image of man, devoid of love and heart, of feelings, of spiritual happiness or catharsis through tragedy. There is the specter of a self-understanding of man in our time that may well be the terminal vestige of the Cartesian monstrosity of a dualism of mind and matter, implying that, in substance, every one of us is nothing but a walking cogito devoid of feelings and love.

In the slowly emerging science of prediction over the past one hundred years or so, it was the economists who displayed a remarkable perception of the significance of pre-conscious formations of the real factor of economy as well as of the role that human drives play in all economic development. To be mentioned here is their constant consideration of cycles that are supposed to be effective in such developments as in the market, currencies, and trade relations. But even in economics, no one seems to know whence such pre-conscious cycles affecting markets come, nor the various degrees of predictability they may or may not allow.

One reason for this is the very variety of cycles economists keep speaking of. There are 2000-year age cycles, 5000-year civilization cycles, 170-year drought cycles; there are stock market cycles of 9.2 and 18.2 years, or 41 or 50 months. According to the Kondratieff cycle, we are now living in the fourth of its five phases, i.e., a phase of collapse that is only to be followed by the transition phase moving toward recovery. A number of explanations for such cyclic causations in market behavior have been proposed, including causations of celestial bodies, of subatomic waves, of harvest and season cycles, or business cycles themselves. In our context, it is interesting to note that economists, who are known to employ linear, objective and measurable times frames, do, in fact, consider the possibility of economic becoming in terms of whatever cycles that are not altogether explainable through calendar time alone. Cyclic understanding of nature has been predominant among human beings over the larger parts of history. Our own present-day linear time frame of looking at the past, present, and future as infinite in both forward and backward direction is relatively recent.

All mythology and religion was beset with cyclic time. One need only mention the long belief in the conjunction of the female cycle and the periods of the moon, which is still expressed in such present-day religions as Christianity, depicting the Mother of God as standing on the crescent moon, or the seasonal character of all life existing in eternal cycles of birth and death, which resembles budding and dying leaves, the spring and fall, of the one tree of life. In religions, conceptions like reincarnation, rebirth, redemption, reenactment, and cyclic recurrences of holidays are only a few of a multiplicity of examples of an ancient experience of time as cyclic.

With at least a partial recognition of the role that cycles and tides play in the market, economists have seen the possibility of there being underneath their projections and forecasts a temporal element other than linear clock-time. And it would appear that the essence of economic prediction, taking into account whatever cycles of life and real factors, must lie in the function of the congruence that economic ideas in a prediction have and share with the approximate segment of the cycle with which the prediction is made. This, however, meets a requirement we mentioned at the beginning. A prediction must not only be concerned with what will or might be in the future. It must equally be riveted and remain riveted in the life of the moment in which it was being made, no matter how far ahead this life-moment has already passed over into the next moment and phase of economic development during the process of the construction of the prediction. In the science of economics, the prediction must be riveted in the segment of the cycle with all its real aspects. While predictions are being made, they must with equal force also look backward at the disappearing life-moment with which they were initially tied up, no matter how the cycle is already turning over into subsequent segments. In this sense, all pre-diction is, and must be, simultaneous retro-diction. Pragmatic prediction is Janus-faced.

Let us now take a less abstract examination of the functionalization of pragmatic truth. Let us take some examples. Whenever a human being draws conclusions or makes inferences according to laws of which he is not aware, insights into essences functionalize themselves.[4] For instance, when we experience something to be false in terms of a rule or a law (such as the law of contradiction) of which we are not aware initially, we suddenly realize that an insight guided our inference. This occurs, for example, in all cases when our conscience begins to pang us without our being aware of laws of preference holding among values. Artists especially have various functionalizing experiences while they create their masterpieces. They do so according to aesthetic laws; however, they are neither aware of them while creating, nor aware of them, even while sketching their art work. In fact, a number of aesthetic laws have been found only after the creations of genuine artists.

The same pertains to the discovery of laws holding in geometry. It does not appear that the first geometricians were aware of the laws hiding among the ratios of the sides of a triangle, or of the circumference of the circle and its diameter. Such laws functionalized themselves while the first geometricians drew lines and circles in the ground with a stick. Overstating the argument, one can say that the respective laws of relations functionalized at the tip of the stick drawing the figures in the ground.

The functionalization of pragmatic truth, and its proving itself in experience, can also find, surprisingly enough, exemplication in religious and moral experience. As far as the former is concerned, the idea of God is neither ante res nor post res, but in mutual condition and function with a cult and all its implications. The ancient Roman praying with closed eyes has a religious experience other than the ancient Greek standing near the seas with arms spread out. The Islamic person kneeling while bending down in rhythms has a religious experience different from the Israeli person moving his body in rhythmic bending. He who kneels while praying has an image of God different from someone who stands while praying. Theological arguments are, for this reason, not alone qualified to determine the essence of religious experience in the individual person. Indeed, overstating a pragmatic view of the experience of the idea of God with its cults, gestures, and postures, one could say that such judgements - as is the case with all syllogistical proofs for the existence of God - hover above the human being without touching him. At least, it does not appear that in practice they have augmented in the past faith in God. It is also in this respect that Pascal seems to have anticipated the above functionalization of the idea of God and of body postures when he said that one should just kneel to learn how to pray to God (PENSÉE, 250).

These cases show us that in religious experience, the idea of the divine functionalizes itself with particular manifestations of bodily experience. It can even be said that among different cultures there are "comparable" postures at and in such experience. There is no doubt that, for instance, a human fist cannot have a praying function. During religious experiences, human hands are rather loosely held over each other or are folded, and unless there is an intense religious imploring involved, the person's hands hardly touch each other, as if they are holding the intangible, divine eternity in them. By contrast, the human fist is directed against something outside of it, be it a state of affairs or even persons. Religious functionalization, therefore, is not related to external objects such as tents, etc., but toward an X of inner perception. For there is an abyss between the functionalization of the idea of the Divine, say, in Dürer's famous Folding Hands, on the one hand, and on the other, the functionalization of the idea of revolution in a communist fist.

As all of the above examples of functionalization would indicate, they imply positive and/or negative values. And as it is the functionalization of moral ideas in particular where values play such a role. In our final example, therefore, the notion of value will be explained as it will also be set forth in what follows.

Let a final exemplication of functionalization, then, be added with regard to that philosophic discipline whose preeminent concern is not so much the presence of being - as is the case with almost all other disciplines in philosophy - but whose concern and objective is what, in the future, ought to be, i.e., ethics. Our starting points are again taken from the quinessential writings, and in this case, from Scheler's monumental work: FORMALISM IN ETHICS AND NON-FORMAL ETHICS OF VALUES. A NEW ATTEMPT TOWARD THE FOUNDATION OF AN ETHICAL PERSONALISM. However, as we did in the previous elaborations, here, too, we do not elaborate on the texts concerned; rather, we go beyond them as far as they pertain to the subject under discussion.

Since Aristotle, and up until Kant and Mill, we are accustomed to expect ethics to provide us with propositions that impart to us the guidelines of how we ought and ought not to act. From ethics we expect propositons that contain the word "ought," pointing to either an imperative or rule that human beings are supposed to be guided by in their dealings with their fellow men, or, as is the case in theft, with objects of fellow human beings. Such imperatives and rules suggest to us a universal validity they may have among all peoples at all times.

Yet, we also know that hitherto no ethics can claim that it has improved the moral status of humanity. Despite the good intentions that the great ethicists undoubtedly reveal, human beings appear to have been equally good and bad. There does not seem to be any diminution of theft, murder, war, or vice, as there is not an increase either of honesty, dignity, or virtue. This state of affairs - so often justifiably mentioned by students of the foundations of ethics - may have something to do with the fact that, on the one hand, imperatives and rules may be quite evidential to human reason and, therefore, be regarded as possibly encompassing all men; but, on the other, imperatives and rules do not take into consideration future historical vicissitudes of real factors.

Despite the immense awe, no doubt, that Kant's "categorical imperative" has on many of us, one cannot help but feel that it does not anymore fit in so well with us today as it might have with people of Kant's own age. This may be because his and other imperatives and rules presuppose that the behavioral grid they cast over all human beings and their future actions could always be followed, regardless of the diversity of cultures, eras, or the accentuation of real factors. For this is the meaning of an imperative, viz. that it is universal, no matter whether one lives in an age of capitalism and technology, or whether one lives in a past era of medieval faith, in an age of myth, or in a future colony on Mars. Both time and space are, implicitly, not contingent upon the meaning of what imperatively, I ought or ought not to do.

Scheler's Value Ethics stipulates that the nuts and bolts of moral imperatives are not all that tight. Indeed, conditions of life and changes in real factors may loosen them quite a bit. His own ethics does not provide us with any imperative. This is because whatever one ought to do, or ought not to do, presupposes the value of what ought to be done, and the disvalue of what ought not to be done. The moral oughtness is, therefore, grounded in values. In addition, since real factors do affect human actions, the moral good shows itself in various cultural colorations, depending on how ideas functionalize themselves with the given life. The moral good, then, is founded in the experience of values.

Our question is, therefore, whether the concept of functionalization pertains to moral ideas and holds in ethics; or, more precisely, is there a process of functionalization in moral experience? In order to show that there is, we utilize an analogy of Scheler's according to which values are analogous to colors in the order of their functional existence.[5]

1. Just as colors are given on surfaces, so also values are given on things, goods, and states of affairs.

2. Just as colors are independent of the thing they color (green can be a tree or water), so also values are independent of what they value (holy can be a god or fetish, or God; comfortable can be an armchair or a bed).

Let us extend this analogy by saying further:

3. Just as there are a few spectral colors, so also are there spectral ranks among all values. These range from the value-rank of the holy down to the spiritual values (beauty in art, justice in law, truth in human cognition), life values, values of usefulness, and those felt only in an organism like comfortableness, etc. These five species of values divide into positive and negative, into values of the person, and those relative life, etc.

4. Just as human sight tends towards seing what is lit up, so also human feeling - in which values are first given - tends toward experiences of ever higher values (in the direction of "love," and ultimately, the "holy").

5. Spectral ranks among values must not be confounded with values of things (for example, the value indicated on a price tag), just as spectral colors may not be confused with factual colorations on surfaces. Value-ranks are graded in the same sense as are spectral colors, no matter how, in practice, we may calculate or manipulate values within their proper ranks. Just as the essence of a color, say, green, has a precise location in the very seeing of it, so also values are given "in" feeling them. The negative value, for instance, of injustice is "felt" very differently from a feeling of pain in the body, etc.

6. Just as spectral colors make possible all visible colors, so also spectral value-ranks make possible practical values. The order of value-ranks is not a choice or a system imposed upon society by reason; instead, the order of ranks among values is constituted by and in the nature of the embodied person and the spectrality of gradations of the person's feelings.

It is crucial for us to realize that among all values and value-ranks mentioned, the moral values of good and evil are not represented. It is this point where the functionalization in moral experiences comes into view. The reason why good and evil (or bad) are not represented is because these values have the nature of absolute becoming in the person. Moral goodness shines through only when a person is realizing a value higher than a value that is just given. All inner propensity toward cultural and spiritual values, for example, make a degree of moral goodness appear in the person because of his inner, emotive preferring these values over lower ones, say, pleasure or profit. Moral goodness is, therefore, an echo resounding the person's good intentions and innermost moral tenor rather than being an object of the will. One may "will" the good also, of course;

however, the terminus a quo of all moral goodness is one's moral tenor from which only the willing of goodness can genuinely occur. Moral goodness is, therefore, of absolute self-becoming, but at the same time mirroring our good intentions and the value-preferrings in us.

All moral goodness that is intended or willed as an object has the temporal character of clock-time and succession. I will it first, then I may realize the good later, and may even receive a reward. But moral goodness as "riding on the back" of an inner moral tenor and tendency toward ever higher values is not of the temporal order of succession; rather it is of temporal order of "duration." Christ's goodness, for example, is absolute becoming in that it suffuses all of His acts and being. Christ does not, and need not, willfully intend to be good - he "is" good. The absolute becoming of his goodness is complete, and therefore holy because all of Christ's phases of existence coincide with the one and only content of his personality: Holiness and Truth.[6] All morally high standing persons, such as Buddha, Socrates, Muhammad, etc., possess a certain radiance of moral value that, like moral goodness itself, is not in the order of clock-time. It is, rather, the very duration of the self-becoming of their person in absolute time that fixes in all future to come their exemplary historical value.

Moral goodness (and evil), then, "functionalizes" itself on the occasion of preferring (or rejecting) values and value-ranks. It is the realization in practice of such positive values as justice, sacrifice, humility, honesty, courage, self-control, the perception and cognition of truth, beauty, and the dignity of human personhood, etc., "with" which moral goodness functionalizes itself. Hence, moral goodness is a transition from lower to higher value-realizations happening in the absolute temporal mode of becoming itself.

I have made the point of the temporal character of moral goodness on various occasions elsewhere and do not wish to elaborate on it further here. But we can, on the basis of the above, now go one step further and say the following: every functionalization of an idea is a self-becoming process. It "becomes" in absolute time. Insofar as pragmatic truth functionalizes itself in conjunction with any kind of work and actions, i.e., cum rebus, it, too, has the temporal character of absolute time.

d) Idea as "Sketch": Introductory Comment

In all foregoing explications of the functionalization of ideas, it was presupposed that ideas are fixed, distinct, and univocal, as well as delineated in themselves. But with such a presupposition, neither the Platonic argument for innate ideas nor the Aristotelian one for abstraction of ideas from things has been debilitated, or even affected, by the pragmatist consideration of the functionalization of an idea in practice.

A theory of knowledge, taking its points of departure from the role of the functionalization of ideas with things in reality, instead of either from inborn or abstracted ideas, cannot, at this point, be seen as a viable alternative to the classical theories concerned, as we claimed a pragmatic view is. For this reason, we must return to some traces of characterizations of human ideas as they can be found in some fragmentary notes of Scheler's later writings and build on them.[7]

An idea of a thing, such as a tent, can neither be distinct nor completely static and clear, when it is maintained that it is neither prior, nor posterior to a thing in perception. It cannot, on this presupposition, bestow on a thing an unconditional and fixed meaning; nor can it be a precise imitation or duplication of the thing it designates. This is also because the idea is said to enter into a function "with" practical experience in which a thing has its roles. Hence, ideas are emergent and becoming, rather than fixed and ready-made concepts that the mind can find before itself if it just looks out for them. If ideas are not fixed and finished, what, then, are they?

Ideas are - and this is more obvious in ideas of prediction - "sketches." An idea is a sketch made in an experience of something the sketch is supposed to prove itself in, and in which this "something," too, proves or does not prove itself, to be true. What is the pristine meaning, we must ask, of a sketch in our context?

Examples of sketches are infinite in number. There are sketches in the sense of outlines or rough plans for the diminution of unemployment; there are sketches in disciplines of art; there are sketches in fashion design; there are sketches of physical theories, and thousands of them on the tables of manufacturers and technologists; there are innumerable sketches in everyday life, when we play or do handicraft, write letters or papers, or plan our schedule for this day or the next one. It belongs to the essence of any sketch that it can be further executed or "filled out" in ever so many ways. In their execution, sketches are changeable, depending on the forces, materials, and real factors with which they are executed toward some kind of completion.

As it can be seen clearly in art, any complete execution of a sketch is at least to some small degree - sometimes invisibly so - short of the original sketch. How often have the great artists destroyed their works because their execution failed to match up to the original sketch - or even betrayed the original sketch. How often do we ourselves discard sketches of letters or papers because they do not vaguely correspond to the initial sketch? A sketch, it seems, tends to both "run away from" its executions (thus making the latter lag behind it) and to invite its execution to be made into it for it to become more complete. All sketches have the character of "running away" and yet still invite us to complete them. They all have this flirtatious ring around them, just as also all predictions do, because, on the one hand, they, too, "run away" from their execution, while, on the other, they are so enticing that they fulfill our instinctive "eagerness to learn." Sketches function like distant constellations of stars, which we fill out with particular contents (astrology).

There exist two extreme cases of sketch and execution or the "filling out" of a sketch. An execution may happen without a sketch in sight, or a sketch may be devoid of execution, being so sparse that it fails to tell us what it is supposed to be. The former case is at hand when a small child scribbles aimlessly on paper, or when we catch ourselves doing the same thing during a long, perhaps boring, telephone conversation. In these cases, there does not appear to be a sketch in the aimless directions of the pen's point. The latter case is at hand when a sketch does not reveal any possible execution, or what any execution might indicate it is of. In this case, we are not able to make out from the disconnected segments and lines of the sketch any meaning. And it might only very slowly dawn on us when its originator begins to slowly filling it out with what he alone knew the sketch was of. Modern art seems to like the two extremes (among others), be it that a painter merely executes by pouring paint on a canvas at random (no sketch), or be it that a painter's sketch is so abstract and objectless that it does not allow of any execution, e.g., when a painting is nothing but a huge black canvas having, at best, an almost unnoticeable bright line near a corner.

It is between these two extremes (of either execution over sketch or sketch over execution) that the essence of a sketch is situated; that is, the functionalization of the sketch with its execution, or possible execution, and vice versa, in practice. The functionalization of a sketch with its execution shows, however, a viable meaning of the term "idea." For the execution must always obey the idea as sketch, while the idea as sketch is also dependent on, or even "waiting for," its execution in practice. The execution, say, of a sketch of a landscape must be one of what is landscapelike, and not one of what is portraitlike. All movements in the executions made are determined by the sketch. But it it also true that a sketch allows of any number of executions and is, therefore, "more" than any of its executions. This is why executions of original sketches are sometimes controversial. We cannot make out whether they are, in fact, the original artist's or made later on by one of his disciples.

Despite a sketch's being "more" than any one of its executions, it remains powerless and impotent- as we said earlier ideas must be - without at least one execution. A sketch torn away from its functional realization in execution has no historical effect. Of course, any drawing of a sketch does contain already a slight degree of execution. But this can be so minimal that no vitality of the sketch is possible. It then remains nothing but a small fragment, much as it may have a concealed meaning in wider, but unknown, contexts. Even in such cases of "ideality" of sketches in pure mathematical, intuitional construction, sketches are lifeless unless they find a way "down" to put their stamp somewhere on the grounds of reality.

From this consideration of the general nature of a sketch, we can make three observations:

1. What Plato called methexis, or the "partaking" between thing and idea, corresponds in pragmatism to the indissoluble functional relation the idea as "sketch" has with its experienced execution in a thing, even when Aristotle equated Plato's methexis with "mimesis," or imitation. Pragmatic truth, along with pragmatic functionalizing ideas, takes into account, in marked contrast to the ancient theories, the temporal element, more precisely, absolute time, which is contained, no matter how covertly, in any action that "works."

2. The functional relation existing between the idea as "sketch" and the execution of it permits us to look at the nature of an historical event or fact from a another angle than the one discussed earlier. We said then that an historical event or a fact always could have happened other than it did, depending on the numerous possibilities of its realization in real factors. This, however, is tantamount to saying that the execution of the historical event can go in

this or that direction; and it can even have no execution when the sketching of an historical event remains without realization. This happens, for example, when a sketch made to reduce unemployment does not work in the given situation. In other words, the role executions play in sketches is the same as the role of the realizations of historical events that can turn out this way or that.

3. The third observation is metaphysical. If the nature of an idea is that of sketching, then we must and can attribute such sketching to all subconscious vital development, down to the self-activity of impulsion and drive-life. The phantasy in impulsion, fanning through all drives, and energizing all perception and mental processes, must contain phantasmic sketches of its own, which we earlier determined to be images or gestalten. But gestalten, too, are sketches. This would imply that in the entire evolution of life as the form of impulsion, the phantasy in impulsion sketched out multiple species of which plants and animal species are only a few traces known to us. Hence, all species known to us are only bits and pieces of the phantasy in universal impulsion; they resemble a few left over hieroglyphs of an ancient inscription. There are many pieces missing in this grand design, perhaps those between man and higher animals. But this does not mean that missing links of the execution of the grand design of life itself are still lying somewhere under the surface of the earth. On the contrary, the grand design of life's phantasy can never be exhausted by any number of its specific executions and realizations. It lies in the essence of a sketch, or in what we called the grand design of universal impulsion, never to be exhaustible in its possible executions.

But with this metaphysical observation made, we have implicitly touched on the question of God. This question must, in our context of a philosophy of prediction, be left aside.

PART IV

THE UNFINISHED IDEA OF MAN

a) Man's Self-Understanding as Sketch

If there were only a grain of veracity in the functionalization between ideas and experience in reality, one could still ask a vital question concerning such a theory. The question is whether or not all sketches in our lives happen by pure fortuity and pure chance. It does not seem that they do: human history, and our own personal lives as well, are always "one" history and "one" life, respectively, showing in each case a continuous sense and meaning that cannot be an outcome of chance, much as chances do occur everywhere.

If we would merely follow what has been said, we would have to expect that all mental sketching, planning, programming, predicting, anticipating, forecasting, and expecting happen, at their initial points of departure or their a quo term, by chance simply because we did not give any account of why they happen in general, nor, let alone, why they happen at a particular time. Whether an idea does or does not functionalize itself in reality seems to be rather fortuitous. It could even be implied that the direction of our lives happens as it does, but not with an inner necessity of character, personality, or outer circumstances. For it was also said, and emphasized that any historical event is open-ended and could have turned out other than it did, this pertaining also to every split second of our lives, which, too, are parts of history. The fortuitousness of the direction of our lives, if it existed in a pregnant sense, would already be seen in our everyday perceptions of things around us, going at a particular moment, say, from seeing a door, then a lamp, then the wall paper, etc., without any inner necessity of our sense of sight jumping or gliding over these things in sequences other than our sense of sight, too, could have allowed them to do.

The same randomness could also be ascribed to what phenomenologists rightly refer to as our "stream" of consciousness, which is replete with an infinite number of acts of the mind. For instance, there does not seem to be a reason why we are thinking now and hating later, willing later or daydreaming now. The very a quo inceptions of such acts seem to be fortuitous because in each case we could have been involved in acts of the mind other than the one that had just been. All this would also imply that the stream of functionalization of ideas with things is replete with a fortuitious nature of inceptions of sketches or ideas so that they happen, as it were, like discrete unpredictible quanta jumps.

But we do not know yet whether act-phenomenology can show us someday in more detail or whether there is, indeed, an inner logic prevailing among all inceptions of acts mentioned above. In general, one refers to such an inner logic as "motivation," which is strictly distinct from "causality." Heidegger, it appears to me, makes a valuable point in contending that there is a logic of the mind as well as a logic of things, both being different from one another.[1]

Our common sense seems to dictate strongly that a total fortuitousness of our lives and history is not acceptable. For all events in individual lives and in history as a whole are not conglomerations of chances; nor are they explainable in terms of causal chains. Approaching the problem in terms of chaos or causality only cannot help us learn about human beings and their history. We suggest that the explanation of absolute time, as we are trying to work it out, is a viable alternative. There is no doubt that the roles of chance and necessity have one-sidedly been overemphasized. Nietzsche, for instance, believes that the essence of the world "dances on chance." For Marx, the knowledge of the world requires a pair of lenses, one lense one-sidedly magnifying social causations, if any, between upper and lower classes, and the other magnifying other economic causations among relations of production, as if ecomonic conditons were the one and only real factor there is in history.

Any investigation into the foundations of the nature of prediction must discard the either-or approach of causal necessity and chance as factors initiating all historical movement and historical processes. Indeed, as long as predictions remain attached to chance or to necessity, or to indeterminism or determinism only, they have no viability in practice. Predictions can also be historically classified under the headings of causality and chance. To this classification, there must be a third choice, which is a viable alternative to causality and chance.

1. If there are only pure chances (Epicurus), there is no prediction possible.

2. If statistical laws prevail throughout chances (Max Planck), qualifiable prediction is possible.

3. If there are only causal laws and neither chance nor statistical laws (Laplace), one could be lead to believe that it is possible for there to be, in principle, perfect prediction and retrodiction.

While No. 1 excludes prediction altogether, No. 3 falsely identifies it with a one-track, cause-effect path on which natural events are supposed to ride. Marx, who was still captivated by classical mechanics and its unlimited belief in predictibility, and without questioning it, even transferred this belief into human history. His own historical predictions, therefore, failed. The only admissible historical validity of prediction is that of quantum physics, or more broadly, that of all statistics which fit "quantifiable" aspects of life. This is the case in medical and social sciences, in the insurance business, and, in part, in psychology, etc. But it also appears that the value of statistics and its forms of predictibility varies, and even diminishes, in other areas. Statistical polls, for example, can be embarassingly wrong. While statistical laws are, in their own right, dependable in atomic physics; while they are rather dependable throughout the natural sciences, medical, social, and psychological sciences, etc., they begin - in Anaximander's sense, as it were - to "pay back" in all nonquantifiable areas of life, where tragedy and death, friction among people and peoples, exchanges of peace and war, where the unfathomable human will, relations among drive-conditioned real factors, and especially occurrences of divine experiences, rare as they are, prevail and may shake and dislodge all historical bearings. But it is precisely these temporal nonmaterial and nonspatial "historical" areas of life where predictions are most enticing and must be scrutinized in their validity. It is in these areas where they are equally challenging and interesting, where they are of much higher importance, if detectable, than in areas of materials and measurable spatial relations. For it is in the "whole" of our practical lives where human beings sketch out projects and projections, and where we ourselves are roughing out our own person at any moment of our lives. Though there are innumerable sketches being made during our lives, it can neither be the case that sketches are fortuitous events, nor that they are based in causal chains underneath them.

For this reason, I propose that all ideas as sketches be reduced to one primordial sketch out of which all ideas and their execution come forth, and by which all of them are guided. This relates analogously to what we mentioned earlier. It was stated that all executions lie well within their sketches determining what the executions are, no matter how many executions there are to a sketch. This primordial sketch, essential to the understanding of prediction, was, I believe, preconceived by Max Scheler. In his PHILOSOPHICAL ANTHROPOLOGY, he argued that all history pivots on those ideas man has of himself, of his self-image or "self-understanding," such as being animal rationale, or an "outcome of evolution," or as a homo faber, a "tool-man." But Scheler did not go a step further to see whether it is possible to reduce these and many more to one idea of man, or as we put it, one original sketch. Let us first see how for us the essence of the human person can be described:

Man is that X which sketches himself.

There are two propositions that follow from this description:

1. There follows the variability of man's self-understanding, for instance, in the East and West, and throughout the ages. The proposition also pertains, and especially so, to every individual person. The person is, at every phase of its existence, a sketch of self happening in absolute time. And, on the basis of our description of the essence of a sketch, our personal executions will always remain behind our self-sketch, always owing, as it were, something to them. For man never knows what he is in his present, but only what he has just been and was.

2. The proposition also implies the person's radical difference from any other entity. If it is the essence of an entity to be able to work itself out, the essence of such an entity must be future-directed. The sketching of self as "futural" would make the past, and all knowledge of the past, only possible, and not vice versa. Our description of man as the only X in the world sketching itself would, paradoxically, imply also that the foundation of all the past lies in the future of man. It must be emphasized that the futural direction of all sketching is not to be confused with projecting something "into" the future. Rather, sketching ourselves is a "becoming" process in absolute time staking out all possible executions that may, or may not, themselves become historical.

We have reached a point where illustrations of types of self-understandings of man in history are in place. We already mentioned the idea of animal rationale, stemming from our Greek heritage, as well as the more modern ideas of man being an outcome of evolution or a tool-man. Another idea of Occidental self-understanding was probably even more effective than these, viz. man as "created being," an idea stemming from the Old Testament. In more recent times, Western man seems to sketch out an idea of himself according to which he is not responsible to God or any transcendence. He begins to understand his existence as "disconnected" from any and all transcendent or transcendental values, implying that he is responsible to no one except himself. His existence is, as Sartre showed, surrounded by nothingness, and the small span in between his birth and death is nothing but his condemnation to freedom in an absurd existence. This atheist self-understanding had its roots in Nietzsche's idea of the "overman," whose historical burden and gravities of the past, including God, will evaporate "beyond good and evil" into the nonmorality of "innocence": this over-humanity, self-reliant and totally devoid of any God-concept and God-need, only occurs during the high noon hour of "eternal recurrence," after which the wheels of life keep on turning new and old transcendent gravities. Nietzsche's eternal recurrence itself is a speculative prediction.

These recent Western ideas have been much cultivated during our century. But equally daring and grandiose as they may be, and notwithstanding their majestic roots in both Ancient Greece and Israel and the Old Testament, they stand no chance to be able to incorporate the Eastern self-understanding. Whereas all Western ideas of man of himself are characterized by action, the Eastern ones are characterized by passive criteria. Above all, there is the idea of the Eastern "sage," whose almost prophetic wisdom must not be confused with the wisdom in Ancient Greece, sophia. In the East, the "homo patiens" is predominant, not a proud homo rationale towering over nature and even challenging the gods. Man is the artist of patience and tolerance. He endures nature, which, in contrast to Western notions, is not all that good. Eastern man does not experience nature as an object, but is "in solidarity with" nature. The Eastern homo patiens is almost the opposite of the Western homo sapiens et rationalis. Patience, enduring, and suffering, and the Eastern art of not resisting pains and evils and permitting them to dissolve themselves are almost unknown in Western sketches of the essence of man. The same pertains to the very executions of the Eastern sketch of homo patiens: the Chinese silent conforming to the "ways" of the Tao; or the clever art and tactic of withdrawing and waylaying the enemy, i.e., not "waging" war, but turning it in favorable directions, without cults of heroship à la Nietzsche and Carlyle, appear almost like an unsolvable riddle in Eastern self-understanding. The passive and tolerant attitude of the East is in marked contradistinction to the restless Western intrusions and explorations into nature made in technology, or made in medical interventions into the organism. Contemporary philosophy has with only few exceptions (Dilthey, Heidegger, Jaspers, Scheler, Spengler) much neglected the mind of the East.

We are also still far away from understanding the lines and styles of executions of Eastern sketches of self-understanding in matters like foreign policy. It is, no doubt, very necessary in foreign policy to understand various cultures in terms of their self-image and self-sketches. This, of course, also pertains to one's own cultural unit. European foreign policies, for example, look at regular American foreign policy as something incomprehensible, if not, naive. This is a result of not understanding the self-sketch and the real geographic and geopolitical factors of both the Canadian and North American peoples, who experience themselves as looking over the Pacific in a westerly direction and over the Atlantic in an easterly direction. For this reason, American foreign policy is much more prone to be more global-oriented than are European foreign policies. The latter are much more compact, interwoven, and at times entangled beyond recognition - as at the beginning of World War I. It is still very difficult for a European, including Russians, to fully understand the fact that America waged the largest two-front war in history, crossing both the Atlantic and the Pacific, with eastern and western fronts covering more than one half of the earth.

No matter how different the ideas of man's self-understanding have turned out to be in East and West, they all resemble "perspectives" of one primordial idea with which philosophy must concern itself in either negating or positing its possibility.

When we referred to such a primordial sketch man must have of himself, this implied that its executions turned out in the East and West in many ways.

It also implies that we still live in an era of very different self-understandings of what and who humanity is. From this angle, one can ask whether humanity as a whole will sometime jump over its perspectival kinds of self-understanding in order to be able to reach a point in which all cultures and civilizations find themselves in balance and mutual understanding. During his final years, Scheler answered this question in the affirmative in the essay entitled "The World Age of Adjustment." Its particular content forms the only prediction in our time made by a philosopher of rank. We do not wish to recapitulate the challenging contents of this essay, which are beginning, no doubt, to bear out their truth. But we should make reference to one point of it. All diplomacy and international law are, within the prediction made by Scheler, to be subordinated to cultural policy and knowledge of culture. Politicians must gain a mutual understanding - no matter how great an effort is needed - of their own, cultural self-understanding. Diplomacy, therefore, presupposes knowledge and expertise of and in culture. For knowledge of culture and of the way of how peoples and civilizations understand themselves in their own sketches is the presupposition for any viable possibility of prediction. Prediction presupposes a full comprehension of the present moment, unfinished as it may be, in which diplomacy is made. But this moment is always part of man's sketch within which human beings act out their existence and exert their projects.

Any prediction of our own futurity at the end of this century also presupposes that we cast light on the still unfinished sketch that present-day man is drawing for himself, and whose lines have already begun to cross well over into the beginnings of the next century. In what follows, we shall deal with an essential component of the present self understanding in the West.

In order to do this, we must take up a contemporary self-understanding that is exclusively of Western origin and has already spread all over the globe: the idea of man in the age of "capitalism."

We shall first present a philosophical account of the essence of what is called "capitalism," and then we will look into its very philosophical foundations insofar as they contribute to focus further on the essence of prediction.[2]

b) Capitalism and the Concept of an Entity

"Capitalism" as a general concept is widely used today in political, economic, and even ideological senses. Only a few thinkers have attempted to seek a foundation for capitalism through pure philosophical reasoning. For such an attempt poses almost insurmountable problems, notwithstanding some positive results that can shed new light on capitalism, its nature, and quintessence.

The concept "capitalism" has rarely been investigated in the literature of one of those thinkers extensively dealing with capitalism, Max Scheler, who was the only European philosopher in this century deeply concerned with the clarification of this phenomenon of our time, not merely in its political ramifications (as, for instance, the Frankfurt School or Marxist theoreticians), but in terms of pure philosophy, that is, without political, economic, or ideological aspects or biases.

The present outline is designed to provide a firsthand look into Scheler's analyses and results. It is not intended to speak either for or against capitalism; nor is it intended to subject capitalism to "rightist," "leftist," "conservative," or "liberal" implications. For the phenomenological researcher, these somewhat emotionally charged starting points would miss the quintessence of the phenomenon under discussion and distort the meaning and role it has in our consciousness.

I have chosen this theme for three reasons:

1. The concept "capitalism" is used rather loosely today, especially among journalists and people who entertain ideological propensities.

2. Max Scheler appears to have been the only European philosopher of our time who tried to understand capitalism. Major thinkers of our century, e.g., N. Berdyaeff, N. Hartmann, M. Heidegger, E. Husserl, K. Jaspers, Ortega, B. Russell, Sartre, Wittgenstein, apparently never tried to do this despite their varied interests in capitalism shown in some of their writings or practical actions.

3. The writings of Scheler on the subject deserve serious attention, notwithstanding the fact that what Scheler tells us seems to have the air of a strange theory. I maintain that Scheler's theory has the air of strangeness because the present usage of "capitalism" is so vague and wide that its appropriate meaning is constantly buried in the mass of global historical events, which become available to us through ever increasingly fast means of communication. This results in frequent superficial usage of words and terms.

Capitalism, Scheler says, spread over the earth like a weed. But this weed cannot be uprooted by way of political or economic systems competing with each other; nor must "capitalism," strangely enough, be conceived as an opposite to "socialism." The roots of capitalism, we are told, go as deep as present-day humanity itself. And with this Scheler suggests that capitalism is primarily a phenomenon to be seen in light of ethics, rather than of economics or politics. Whatever the affiliations capitalism may have with any of the latter areas of knowledge, it is important to realize right from the beginning that such affiliations are not of primary importance. Without making any specific reference to "phenomenology" (briefly stated, the investigation of any and all processes of consciousness in their being co-related and founded in the ultimate meaning of "world" in terms of temporal fluxes of infinite meanings consciousness is "of"), Scheler implies everywhere that "capitalism" rests on a specific attitude of consciousness; in other words, on a disposition or bearing of consciousness and on a particular state of mind or mind-set, as it were, characteristic of our civilization. This attitude makes things around us appear in a specific fashion. If this is true, or only partially true, a second point can be seen in Scheler's theory, namely, that capitalism cannot be a concept pertaining to one specific social "class": properly understood, capitalism is indifferent to, and independent of, any class-consciousness, class-theory, or social classes. Let us take a close look at the fabric of capitalism as it occurs in our conscious awareness and, consequently, history.

In speaking of a "capitalistic state of mind," Scheler wants to indicate that all entities, i.e., all things and states of affairs, present themselves to the mind in terms of their possible or actual capitalizability. Things settle around us, telling us, as it were: "See what you can do with us so that you can get something out of us," or "See what my usefulness is to you and if there is none, then discard me."

But the way things are "given" to us in this fashion remains, for the most part, unnoticed. This is why human beings can have the belief that things given in this fashion present themselves in perception and/or to the mind, as they supposedly "really" are or as they are "objectively." All objectivity of this kind is, however, relative to the attitude the mind has toward them and must not be confused with that objectivity which some philosophers claim can be established in the absence of a state of mind - as, for example, a number of Husserlians claim, asserting that the phenomenological "primary impression" is retrievable despite its implicit noetic meaning-input (Eindeutung). We put this problem aside. What phenomenologists and others call "attitude of mind" (Bewusstseinseinstellung) is well known. But this attitude by which and in which we are conscious of something has hardly been seen in its its historical function that Scheler has in mind when he speaks of capitalism as a way in and through which all entities tend to present themselves to the ordinary human being in a peculiar, capitalizable perspective.

Let us recall by way of three examples what "attitude of consciousness" can mean before we try to further elucidate the meaning of capitalism. Let us stay within ordinary, everyday experiences because our study is not concerned with complex phenomenological noetic-noematic technicalities pertinent to such attitudes. Such highly technical aspects would yield very little in regard to the very historical significance that we intend to address. Let a "table" be used in the three following examples, which exemplify different "attitudes of consciousness."

1. A carpenter who sees a table or wants to build one sees it under the aspect of something that can be made or crafted. If he makes a table and spends a good deal of craftsmanship on it, he may show a certain amount of pride, which, in the past, betokened genuine craftsmanship. In this first example, the value of the table is constituted by the work put into it. The carpenter may even be hesitant to sell its quality. If he does wish to sell it, however, there are three possibilites for the price he may set: a) he can set the price so that he can make a profit, b) he can set the price so that he takes a loss, for example, selling it for less than its value to a close friend, or giving it away as a present, and c) the price can be set such that it is proportionate to the work he put into it, or set in the closest possible correspondence to the amount of work. In the latter case, the price set is tantamount to the medieval justum pretium, the just price, i.e., "just" with respect to effort and work. As it is well known, canonical opposition to paying interest(s) rests on the concept of justum pretium; but the just price theory also plays a role in modern wage conflicts between unions and corporations, employees, and employers, etc. Either side of the negotiating table claims to have the formula for a just price for work done, i.e., for the just wages or salaries. And it may well be the case that either side is right (conflicting as the views may be, leading at times to strikes) because of the attitude within which the phenomenon under discussion presents itself "objectively" to both sides of the negotiating table.

One more remark must necessarily be made in this context. Marx, and most forms of socialism after him, claimed that the justum pretium idea must be realized by human work and endeavor. Historically, however, this idea is derived from Heraclitus (c. 540-480 B.C.), for whom all things are in the process of transformation and exchange, including "wares for gold and gold for wares" (Fragment DK 90). In this conception, the wares containing the work spent on them, and the remuneration "gold," are not regulated by humans, but by the X called Logos, i.e., that which holds together (legein: to collect) and gathers into one cosmos all opposites (including economic ones) and holds shifting opposites together. For all opposites in nature and history require each other in order to exist, i.e., without one term of a pair of opposites (in our context, the opposite party at the negotiating table), the other term in that pair is meaningless and has no existence of its own. Opposites, Heraclitus might say today, regulate themselves or must be deregulated from any artificial and technical human interference as much as possible so that they can "float," as the well-known economic expression calls it. It may well be that modern man is too impatient, too restless, to be able to put some trust into this, and for this reason, remains too arduously preoccupied with technical endeavors that he thinks can improve the world.

2. The aforementioned table may be given in quite another fashion, namely, in the eyes of the artist. "His" table is characterized by the fact that the table appears in the fashion it "could" have been, but in reality is not; or the table appears as it "ought" to have been (in the painting). The painted table is different from the real table. The real table appears to be "less" than its artistic representation. In reality, that which the table is not "is" in the painting of it. The painted table is "more" than and different from, the real table because the artist's attitude toward the table is what it should or could be. He puts something "into" the table, which to him is more "truthful" than the real table. The difference between the painted table and the real table is also aimed at in artistic photography, understood as a mechanical art that

represents the table in a fashion that also reveals a difference between the real table and its photograph. Indeed, both photography and the art of painting can represent the table in such ways that the real table is not recognizable anymore, as is the case in certain kinds of modern art. In short, for the artist, the table is not given as something to be crafted, but as something to be "created."

3. There is a third way, among others, to whom a table can be given. Let this pertain to a businessman selling tables and furniture. For him, the table is given as an object of profit and not as something to be crafted or created. In fact, the table's very existence may be accessible to him only through bills, numbers, computer data, without even seeing the table in any detail - if at all. It may even lose its "tableness," as it were, because it may "dissolve" into all other furniture in the store and the stock selling better than it. In this example, the table is given to a "calculating" mind.

It is characteristic of our age of technology that the existence of something begins to become more and more evanescent because it is more and more artificially translated into numbers, symbols, or computer printouts. One tends to believe in them more than in the factual existence of things reflected in them. If there are discrepancies between the data and the factual state of things, one tends to adjust the state of affairs of things rather than to adjust the computerized data to the state of affairs of things. In a way, the existence of the object is expected to conform to the computer because it is manageable in the computer. It remains to be seen whether this general tendency - if it holds as stated - is a dangerous self-deception that modern society has unknowingly subjected itself to. A common joke goes: computer data are right, only the weather is wrong. This and other similar computer jokes may well betray a deep-seated self-deception, blind belief, and wishful thinking characteristic of a society that is emotionally occupied, if not obsessed, with technical equipment.

What the above three examples of a possible

giveness of an object imply, however, is something more significant than the examples would indicate: what in phenomenology has traditionally been called "consciousness-of-something" (the fact that whenever our consciousness is in a wakeful state - including dreaming "of" - it relates to meanings of inner and outer objects-including consciousness being "of" itself in self-reflection) must have its foundation in what I call "consciousness-out-of." We are not aware of this out-of, i.e., the attitude or mind-set that places an object (table) into a particular sketch as, for example, something to be made, created, or sold. Even a reflection on this "out of" (as we are just doing) would have to come from another "out of" from which our consciousness comes to reflect, and so on in an infinite regress.

I, therefore, suggest that all "consciousness of" (Husserl) is, in the order of foundation, based on and preceded by a "consciousness-out-of," from which all that which consciousness is "of" receives attitudinal determinations. This thought would put Husserl's well-known "consciousness-of" and intentionality on the level of constitutions (Bewusstseinsleistungen) that are only second to a consciousness out of which something is given in attitudinal characteristics; at the same time, this implies that we can never be sure whether or not the phenomenon of a meaning, or the meaning of a phenomenon, in our mind is given in "itself," i.e., without attitudinal aspects. This "itself" must necessarily remain concealed.

While I realize that this proposal gets at the very nerve of Husserl's entire enterprise, it may well be supported by further research. For it may well be the case that whereas language allows for the expression that we are always conscious "of something," it does not allow for an expression like we are conscious "out" of something, precisely because this "out" does not pertain to a "something" or an entity it could be aware "of" (Husserl's consciousness). The "out-of" pertains to the form of existence entities may have or assume for us; however, this "out-of" (for instance, that of the carpenter, artist, and businessman) conceals the very Being of entities because it does not address itself to entities in a manner the consciousness of "something" does. The "out-of" is tantamount only to a clearing, or opening, setting a possible sketch for entities to be so, or other than so. The fact that both Heidegger and Max Scheler argued against Husserl's primordiality of the ego, because to both of them the ego is derivable (for the early Heidegger from "Dasein," for Scheler from "Person"), may well be explainable in terms of my proposal.

Our three examples, of course, make reference only to three individual consciousnesses concerned. What about an attitude that prevails over a larger group of people, or even a civilization or a culture? This is the case, so Scheler argues, with the "capitalist" mind, the kapitalistischer Geist. It is through this mind-set, hidden behind all consciousness-of, that everything is seen under the aspect of profitability, capitalizability, and usefulness. The capitalist mind is not restricted to classes as if expressing only social and sociological conditions. Not only the "rich" are capitalists, but all human beings of our time are, to larger or lesser degrees, "capitalists." This includes, a fortiori, socialism. Socialism seeks to represent a particular class within the capitalist mind. Spiraling wage demands, for instance, are as profitable to the individuals concerned as are certain corporate profits to business leaders and industrialists. In the former case, one might speak of micro-capitalism; in the latter, better-known case, macrocapitalism. But in the theory of capitalism before us, it is not the amount of profit that characterizes capitalist man: it is the quality and type of mind-set at hand that determines the conduct of human beings and the role they play in society. For this reason, we must qualify the aforementioned three examples in terms of this capitalist mind prevailing today. Both the carpenter as a total craftsman and a near-ideal artist lost in the beauty of his creations do not exist in the age of capitalism because a poor carpenter, too, crafts the table and does it for profit and more profit.

Artists, too, do not live in the world of their creation anymore, but in the practical world promising success. They, too, live in a world of technical reproduction of their creations and in a world of public recognition, which is much needed for their success as well. Both the craftsman and the artist hold objects within a capitalist view, a view that grows into and around their objects like a weed in the world of competition.

To argue, for instance, that capitalism is an outcome of an age within which and "out of which" both traditional economic capitalism and socialism must be understood amounts to an impressive observation Scheler provided. For it results in an equally impressive consquence and commands that both traditional capi- talism and socialism are to be rejected and not to be taken as terms, for or against, by which we make political and economic decisions. It is the idea that man has of himself, as homo capitalisticus, Scheler once said, that contains morally unacceptable traits. Without going into any detail of the moral implications involved, one of the major unacceptable traits of man's self-understanding today is the fact that machinery, technology as a whole, fascinates man to the extent that the value of the individual person - despite all the talk about preserving it - is being threatened in a relentless struggle for technical progress, success, and advancement. It is being threatened by the unexamined belief in computer technology that all the difficulties we have in solving problems stem from insufficient data - until, years from now, it will be noticed that massive collection of data will have created at least as many problems as the computer perhaps could have solved.[3] It is, therefore, the misplacing of the value of the person "under" the value of what is useful and productive that is unethical. There is not less "capitalism" in socialism than there is in capitalism itself.

Since capitalism is concerned with entities and their facet of capitalization, we must look into the nature of an entity, lest our treatment of capitalism hangs in the air. Philosophical, albeit brief, considerations of an "entity" are also necessary insofar as all predictions pertain to the incipient behavior of entities and states of affairs.

What, then, is an entity or a thing? They are, for instance, tents, tables, mountains, oceans, stars, money, animals, buildings, clouds, plants, utensils, and any state of affairs, such as social, economic, personal ones. I propose the following classification:

An entity, or a thing, can be spatial and/or temporal:

1. All visible things, for instance, are spatial. A die with its dots one to six fills out a space on the table. It is in the space of the room.

2. An entity can also be both spatial and temporal. All states of affairs are of this nature. States of affairs pertinent to relations of property, for example, are partly spatial because the real estate concerned extends over ever so many square feet. But it is also temporal because its value changes in time. Or, in atomic physics, a particle is either spatial and/or temporal (wave), depending on the way the experiment has been set up.

3. An entity can also be only temporal. This is the case with, say, a sound coming from a harp or the pitch of a voice. A sound is not a thing like a cube or die lying on the table before us.

The more an entity is temporal the less there is a justification, I hold, to refer to it as an object. Object literally means that something is "thrown against" and stands before us. But all acts of the mind such as thinking, willing, etc. are not "objects." They are processes having the character of becoming and unbecoming, and they are not in space.

The above three facets of entities are always tied to a fourth one that has been discussed since Pythagoras and Aristotle. For all entities also occur in "forms" of their being. These forms of being are mostly referred to as "categories" and have been investigated again and again, especially since Aristotle, up to Kant and more recently by N. Hartmann.

The word "category" has two roots, and literally

means "down onto" (cata) and the "market" (agora). The ancient Greek philosophers often taught in the open, under the blue Mediterranean skies, in the marketplace of Athens, which is well preserved to this day. They stood on a step and in this way taught and spoke "down unto" their students and all Athenians interested. To this day, professors teach from lecterns while standing, much as this noble tradition is challenged today in the name of a peculiar understanding of democracy in which all are to be "socially levelled" and consequently made equal. Classroom design and modern furniture contribute to the teacher sitting on the same ground level as their students do. The teacher is expected to be a primus inter pares, and not to talk "onto" his students and audiences. Seating arrangement is also at times circular so that the teacher is surrounded by them. This tendency, however, wholly miscontrues our educational heritage. The elevation of a teacher or speaker does not imply that he speaks "down onto" people. The Greek "cata" has no social or unsocial implication. On the contrary, the "down onto the marketplace" is precisely what modern seating arrangment wishes to convey: the primus inter pares, but in the sense of the teacher's visibililty by all, and all people's own visibility to their teacher. Teacher, student, and people, in the Greek understanding of democracy, are in the presence of truth (a-lethia) and are in roles that entities play in their city. The Greek word for city is polis, which, as Heidegger showed us, is related to polos, meaning a "pole."[4] In essence, the "agora" is the pole around which entities of the city, polis, settle. And it is the teacher, or any best man among the people, who can and should stand on the step and tell of the truth that unconceals itself to man. Greek democracy is, paradoxically, aristocratic; that is, it provides the forum for the best (aristos). Scheler once said in this sense of democracy that the greatest mistake any democracy could ever make would be to lock out an elite;[5] and we add: to lock out an elite for the sake of unconditional equalitarianism. The term "category," then, does not only imply the controversial "down onto" alone. For without the marketplace itself, and all the people in it, the "down unto" is senseless. Hence, it is the audience and the students that are equal contributors to the function of eduction. They, too, are in the light of truth much as their teacher guides them. There is no "down onto" without its opposite "looking up to." This also pertains to all entities that are said to belong to categories. Categories are of an imperial nature because they "impart" classifications onto things while things must be there for this impartation or imperial rule of the categories. Instances of categories are that the things can be "real," "unreal," "valuable," "true," "ideal," "nonexistent," "becoming" (which for us is "the" category); things can be "causal," "statistical," "necessary," and whatever forms there may be in which things appear.

However, what philosophers have always referred to as the "Being" of entities is not an entity and therefore is not object of ordinary and everyday thinking, although "Being" does play a role in all entities and their relations. What is this role? Let us answer this question in terms of use of language. In everyday phrases like "It is nice weather today," "It is four o'clock," "God is," "God is not," "Business is good," we use the word "is" as a form of "to be." But we also use this word when it is not said, for example, when we say: "O.K.," "Nice job," or simply "Fantastic." This would indicate that the verb "to be," and its forms like "is" or "are," is different from any other verb or noun in that verbs and nouns are always of entities. "Tree" as a noun refers to an entity. "To grow" refers to the growing of the tree as an entity. But "to be" does not refer to a particular entity, in contrast to "to run," "to ride," "to act," or in contrast to nouns like "home," "rock," "cloud." When taken by itself, the verb "to be" seems to be empty. It does not predicate anything of any entity or state of affairs. This indicates that "to be" or "being" is not an entity at all and, therefore, it is no thing, or "nothing." Let us illustrate what we just said:

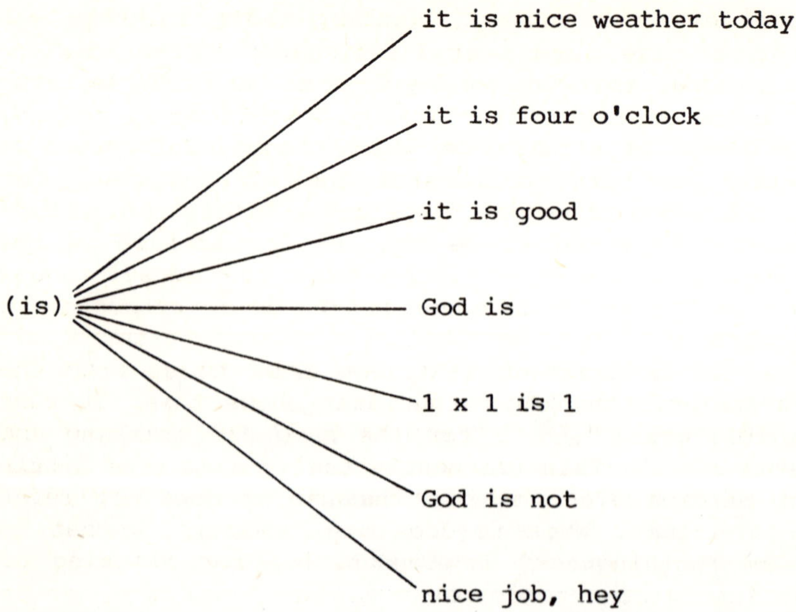

On the right side of the graph, the word "is" is always of something, of an entity. But on the left side, the "is" is not. That is, it is pure Being. Nevertheless, it is always presupposed when we speak, no matter which language we speak. But we are not aware of this function of "is" or "to be" while we speak. Its function remains concealed. After all, we want to say "something" and not nothing. Nonetheless, any sentence spoken would be unutterable without this "is." Indeed, the concealment of this "is" or "to be" makes the sentence possible and unconceals what is being said, no matter whether what is said is true, false, good, bad, etc.

However, the "to be" must not and cannot be taken as an object as we just did in our description. To think the "to be" itself cannot be described, but requires thinking proper, i.e., philosophical thinking as it was, for example, revealed in pre-Socratic philosophy. For the pre-Socratics did not at all "think" in terms of modern concepts like object, entities, and subject. Rather, their thinking was original, i.e., not everyday discursive thinking.

Everyday thinking is discursive. We think in terms of going through (dis-cursively) relations, things, and states of affairs. We weigh things, deliberate on them, and form judgements and syllogisms. But thinking proper is not discursive. In essence, philosophical thinking is be-ing. It is implicit in the previous concept we introduced, the consciousness "out of," that it does not refer, as we stressed, to an entity.

A famous fragment that came down to us from the pre-Socratic thinker Parmenidies shows this. It runs as follows: ". . . for the same are thinking and being . . ." This fragment actually says very little (or perhaps even nothing) because it does not refer to entities. What it does say, though, is that to think "nothingness" is impossible, for thinking or mentioning it already makes nothing something, or an entity, viz. something in the thought of it. Hence, thinking and being are the same, actually synonymous, if we could only so harshly and radically suspend everyday dis-cursive thinking as the pre-Socratics did. For in all talk, saying, deliberating, dreaming, in short, in all activity of the mind, the "is" is hiddenly implicit. To use an expression of pure thinking: thinking "is-es" since the is-ing is in all articulation, no matter whether we use the word "to be" or any of its various grammatical forms, or not.

In all entities, then, and in all thought of them, the "being" or "to be" is present, albeit hiddenly so. This we must keep in mind when any idea man has of himself is seen as a sketch that is being filled out with executions in, and relating to, entities.

This brief discussion of the Be-ing of entities cannot be pursued here any further. But even in its brevity, it helps us to bring into an order the concepts used in this part of our investigation of prediction, viz. the concepts of idea as "sketch," the concept of consciousness "out of," and the concept of "entities," in their relation to Be-ing. The order for us must be the following:

1. Consciousness "out of" is the subjective side

occurring in the mind, of Be-ing, which, in turn, would have to be referred to as the objective side of consciousness "out of." But for reasons not concerning us here, it is imperative not to use terms like "objective" and "subjective." For our purposes, I introduce the terms "convex" and "concave," asserting that consciousness "out of" is concave, it being impossible "to be" without its convex, Be-ing and vice versa.

2. It is from this ontological relation existing between pure thinking and pure Be-ing that ideas in the sense of "sketches" are possible. All sketches are "of" something, viz., of entities. Entities are the material for all possible executions of a sketch. Sketches are also comparable to "attitudes" of the mind, or mind-sets, projecting outlines and specific looks entities assume in such attitudes.

It is the projective outlines of sketches qua ideas that are the essence and nucleus of all prediction. Sketching, or having ideas, is projecting. Projecting is forseeing how entities will, or will not, conform to what is foreseen in projecting, while projecting itself runs down and along the lines of sketching.

The essential nucleus of prediction fits well within what we said earlier. Ideally, sketching always implies degrees of execution. One sketches "with" degrees of executing the sketch, or, sketches are cum rebus, with things. True, a sketch is a sketch. It is unfinished and awaits some kind of completion. But there is no sketch, no matter how unfinished it may be, unless its initial points forming infinitessimally small lines are "becoming" something, an entity, lest the sketch remains a meaningless scribbling. The sketch may or may not find its functional executions of more or less degrees of completion and understanding. In this sense, all ideas that do not "work," remain what they are: they remain unrealized, and in the mind only, without finding expression and, in practice, without corroboration. Such ideas staying aloft, as it were, are numerous and we may underestimate the times of their occurrences in our lifetime.

c) Variations of the Functional Appearance of Entities and the Role of the Sketch

In the preceding section, we stated that entities are spatial and/or temporal. The philosophical term "entity" refers to both things and states of affairs. The latter application of the term pertains to capitalism. Capitalism is, as a state of affairs, an entity. It is both spatial and temporal. It is spatial because one of its foundations are material things. It is temporal because it represents an historical era having a peculiar mind-set revealing the peculiar self-understanding of the generations living in it.

The example of a table given in three ways to three different people was to illustrate that entities can appear in terms of facets such as styles, tones, modes of expression, functional use, trends, profits, beauty, crafts, etc. They always manifest what we can now call variations of the functional appearance of an entity, depending on the particular mind-sets at hand.

We are also now in the position to extend the argument of variations of functional appearance into larger scopes and periods of history. For the way all entities can appear to whole peoples and civilizations must be in relation to the mind-set to them. Let us take a second look at this in order to gain further insight into our present-day sketch of the world as reflected in our mind-set, i.e., a better look at the essence of the capitalist sketch. It is from this basis that we may better be able to reflect upon the facets of our own world without bias, because we will be able to trace a number of differences between the capitalist world and any other possible variation of the world and its entities.

The method of comparision may be permissible in this case because it is hardly, if at all, possible to bring into focus one's era while living in it without such comparison. Comparisons seem to be the best accesses to it. For there is no question that the way we see ourselves now, or the ways all of us living at the end of the century will look upon the world, will soon be seen differently by others and future generations. They will look back at our decade as something that for them will have already passed, but which for us is now present.

Not only phenomenologists and historians, but also pragmatists like W. James and G.H. Mead, pointed out again and again that all reflections into the past inevitably modify the past because it must be seen through the windows of the present. Whether we can ever see the past the way it was experienced by those who lived in it at the time is a major question of hermeneutics. This includes our own personal past, which, too, is different now from what it was while it was experienced as a present in the now past. And we stated at the beginning that the answer to this question - pertaining as it does to history, diplomacy, politics, law, psychiatry, eduction, bibilical researchers, all of which essentially related to what was a state of affairs in the past - must imply full cognizance of absolute time and the role it plays, individually and collectively, in the sketching out of ideas and in the becoming un-becoming events concerned. For absolute time, we saw, runs like a thin, unnoticeable thread through the three dimensions of time, the past, the present, and the future, connecting them like a cobweb would connect three distant corner in space.

It is of particular importance in this connection to realize always that prediction, too, must pass through the windows of any present it is made in. Indeed, predictions made in the presents of centuries ago do, in fact, betray the styles, fashions, ways of thinking of the then present; in short, they betray variations of respective appearances of entities of a present that has now passed. An exception of this seems to be a prophecy. In prophecy, the very destiny of human beings is at stake, say, the chosen or the unchosen, life or death. These are divined as something that does not admit of any qualification of a present. Indeed, biblical prophecy can be so strong an undercurrent in history that it is experienced in any present without qualification. A reflection of this, for example, are forms of Calvinism that touch any moment of those living in either the present present, or past or future presents.

The present plays a substantial role in all prediction-making. It stands to reason that in a mythological variation in the appearance of entities predictions are very different from those made in a capitalistic society. In essence, all predictions made throughout mythological eras have as their center values of life, i.e., values of what is noble or ignoble, what is supportive of life or what calls for death. Homer's ILIAD and ODYSSEY are only a few examples concerned. In mythology, all entities show themselves to be suffused with spirits, deities, or demons of all kinds. Spring, for instance, is expressive of Demeter's joy over once again seeing her daughter Persephone, who was held hostage by Hades; fall and winter express Demeter's sorrow over having to surrender Persephone again to the underworld. Demeter was the sister of Zeus and the goddess of agriculture. In ancient Rome, she was called Ceres, from which our word cereal is derived. The theophantic appearance of entities allows of little or no causal explanation of natural events because everything is dependent on the wills or moods of gods or demigods. Causes, let alone scientific ones, were hardly present in the ancient world. The Greek word aitia testifies to this nicely, because it means both cause and guilt. The question "why" something happens (cause) was no more important that the question of "who" made something happen, or was guilty of this or that. By contrast, in our time such "who" explanations of events in nature occur only in fairy tales, and have no scientific justification for us. Entities are objects to be calculated, explored, and utilized with programmed effects. They are to be related in terms of cause-effect relations so that, one hopes, predictions can be made with scientific stringency. Man's self-understanding is characterized by his own potential and actual "mastery" over nature. He needs no gods and their wills in this. God, so runs the overused phrase, is dead, meaning man understands himself as above nature and as holding on firmly to all things he invented to keep nature under control and expand this control without limits.

This idea of man as a master over nature is substantially different from the Asian Indian ethos. In this ethos, entities are neither theophantic nor pragmatic. Throughout the history of India, entities are felt as an organismic whole, i.e., as the totality of nature itself in which and with which - and not above which - man lives. In the Indian ethos, there is very little tendency to "master" nature. Indeed, there exists such a degree of emotive identification and co-feeling with the whole of nature, including human nature itself, that technology has a counterpart in Indian culture: the psychic techniques having the aim of overcoming life's sufferings. In the Asian Indian self-understanding, man is not opposite, but "in" nature, living along with it. In one word, man's sketch represents a total solidarity with all nature. This entails an interesting consequence. The human ego is no subject of philosophical investigation. Rather, it is less articulated and to be dissolved. By contrast since Descartes, the ego has been a major object of investigation of western philosophers. For some, it has even been regarded as the essence of human existence, much as some, like Nietzsche, Heidegger, and Scheler attributed only very little importance to it. But these are only exceptions to a general Western trend that again and again culminated in various thinkers such as Fichte, Kant, Freud, or Husserl. As seen from an Asian mind-set, the intense occupation with the human ego appears almost pathological. In the East, man's existence is here determined by the resistance of the whole human being over against nature. And resistance implies suffering. And the only way to nip suffering in the bud is by reducing and eliminating not the ego, but resistance itself. And this does not require methods; it requires psychic techniques.

A summation in our context of the Oriental self-understanding implies even more carefully worded generalized statements. The Western understanding of the Oriental sketches of man and the world leaves much to be desired. Scheler once said that the West has been taking itself too seriously and overestimating its importance; it is time, Scheler thought, for the West to study the East.

Looking into research done in this area, there seems to be a view emerging that especially the Chinese culture is more akin to the West than the Indian one is. Many translations of ancient Chinese texts, among them those of Chuang-Tzu and Lao-Tzu, reveal on their surface a surprising affinity to ancient Greek philosophy, in particular, to the pre-Socratic thinkers. It may be the case that we read such translations through Western glasses. Yet, one cannot help having the impression that the Tao reminds one of Anaximander's formless primordial stuff or of Hesiod's Chaos (abyss) producing the first types of entities such as love or air (Anaximenes), or of the theory of the atomists holding that life and death are degrees of the condensation of primordial stuff, or of the idea of a self-active world-mind (Anaxagoras), or of the eternal transitions taking place from young to old, life and death, sleep and wakefulness, and vice and versa (Heraclitus and Chuang-Tzu). On the other hand, we do not find in Greek thought something similar to the notion that the Tao (qua Being) both is and is not, much as this Tao is "unsayable" as is the Logos of Heraclitus. But Tao is also said to be temporary and that its Yin (dark) and Yang (bright) are not entities, thusly defying what in Western thought is known to be the ontological difference. Heidegger discovered, however, that the Greek Alethia (qua Truth/Being) is itself "polemic" and replete with strife within itself, which certainly reminds one of the Yin and Yang in the Tao.[6] Perhaps the Yin and Yang are more difficult to comprehend than the Tao, in the same way as the concealment-unconcealment in the Alethia may be more difficult to comprehend in Heraclitus and Parmenides.

Whatever these Chinese metaphysical notions bespeak, it is, most importantly, the self-understanding of man himself that is quintessentially different from that of Western sketches. For it is the Oriental followship or free following to a "master" who gives artistic and intuitve advice penetrating the persons following him that belongs to the core of Oriental life. These masters are equally luminous, sagacious, and knowledgeable in the inimitable art of intersubjective, psychic dialogue. Their techniques have no methods, net results, or bottom lines; they are equally powerful and personal, not having calculable cash values or purposes of profitable success, if they are genuine.

We do not have to pursue this discussion of variations of the appearance of entities any further at this point. Let us remind ourselves of the steps that our investigation into the essence of prediction has taken. We proceeded from 1) the explication of absolute time and on to 2) the nature of the essence of life as impulsion and the role of drives as they revealed absolute time to us, and 3) the pragmatic functionalization of ideas qua sketches in reality and the notion of the sketch itself, as well as 4) to the nature of entities insofar as all prediction pertains to entities.

These steps were not to provide any proposal of what the future might look like; rather, they were to pinpoint essential components in the essence of prediction, components, that is, that any prediction-making must take into consideration if it is to fulfill at least in part its explicit purpose in a commensurate way.

In order to bring together these points and articulate the metaphysical message implied, I wish to avail myself of an analogy, thereby avoiding what otherwise might command elaborations too long for our subject: just as the physics of technology has provided us with the spectacular view of the earth as it is seen from the surface of the moon, with its typical blue, white, and, at times, reddish colors-inviting both our awe and humility as we look at this tiny habitat of ours existing on the vast and dark background of outer space - so also our implicit metaphysics provides us with a view of man living on this earth, sketching ever so many ideas of himself along with their numerous, colorful variations of cultures and entities that cover the planet, but existing on the vast and deep background of life's impulsion and absolute time.

Granted that ideas are sketches functionalizing themselves only when they are of a pragmatic meaning in reality, thusly existing only in their possible executions; and granted, too, that the human mind itself exists only in its functionalization, with life being its conduit for the mind's sketches (personalization of the mind in absolute time), it should become clear that the very roots of capitalism, as understood to be one facet through which entities reveal themselves in a particular manner, are neither political nor economical. Politics and economics are only few strokes in the execution of an underlying self-sketch that do not at all exhaust the sketch as a whole. No execution of a sketch, we saw, can do so. Therefore, the capitalist sketch is that "out of" which capitalistic executions ensue. Hence, a metaphysics of capitalism, we saw, can show that capitalism - as any other mind-set - is related to Being. Its entity-character consists only in the fact that any sketch must in its own inception always imply degrees of its own execution. In drawing a sketch, I simultaneously execute it.

In itself, a capitalist sketch is not necessarily a bad one, as we might have at times suggested. Man is free to control all powers of nature if they can serve his life. In this, we are not only thinking of the famous biblical passage concerned, but also referring to positive accomplishments of capitalism so often underestimated or even forgotten. The invention and marketing of penicillin saved millions of lives, to mention only one such accomplishment.

But the capitalist mind-set begins to assume a touch of vice, and perhaps the greatest of them all, whenever it trespasses its proper borders serving and benefiting human life. The relentless search for more and more technical control and capitalizabilities is frequently not shared by the younger generation. Excessive executions of so-called work ethics throughout all occupations, relentless cravings for success, limitless competition, and plethoric production and surpluses are only a few weeds that trespass all too far the proper application of the value of usefulness. The capitalist ethics of utilitarianism is, within its own right, a viable ethics.[7] The more recent work ethic, however, did not stop short of declaring anything under the sun to be a target of potential or actual technical controls, capitalizability, and marketability. Ever new markets are opened up, as the expression pointedly says, but not only markets to be found on the surface of the earth. Outer space is as much seen in the facet of controlability and marketability as is the market emerging in the cybernetics of genes allowing of an ominous production of human beings - as entities - tailored to preferred types of human persons. But the most ominous capitalist excesses of controlability and capitalizability has as its target in the marketing of human salvation, ranging from payable indulgences in the past to present-day banking accounts bulging beneath religious phraseologies of certain righteous preachers, televangalists, or even gurus.

The previous lines were intended to come across a little harshly in order to properly recall how very different, in essence, the aforementioned Asian sketch of world and self is, no matter to which degrees socialism and capitalism infiltrate the Asian continent. We hold that this infiltration will not succeed in the manner Western entrepeneurs might wish it could. This is because the active infiltration runs counter to the enigmatic and passive presence of entities in the Chinese culture and the Indian identification and solidarity with nature. Japan appears to be only a partial exception to this. For its own capitalism did not do harm to the Japanese self-understanding. The strong functions of masters mentioned earlier is reflected, for instance, in their "communal" management in factories, showing strong organismic rules among employers and employees rather than mechanical, artificial, or even militarist ones found in Western management. Japanese management is not regimental, but communal; this perhaps is one reason for its continued success.

In capitalism, all entities appear as objects to be worked with and on, to be programmed or manipulated. Entities are experienced almost exclusively in their spatial controlability and manageability. Their temporal characters tend to be translated into spatial representation on screens for easier understanding. Precisely this, however, runs counter to the Asian mind. If it is true that man's self-understanding or self-sketching is the ultimate vehicle driving forth all historical action on this globe, one can see that both economic and political capitalism qua socialism do not "fit" into the Asian understanding of the human being, much as capitalism has been advancing in Asia. China may turn out to be the classic example for this because its Marxism has already yielded to the executions of the sketch of the Chinese genius of mind. And we can even add modern art - bespeaking so well the controlling, managing sketch of capitalism - in that it largely consists in the dexterity and technical mastery of skillfully handling and perfecting paint and brush and their usage, of "creating" materials in the plastic arts. Especially the technical mastery of strings and keys passes as art - at times a display of manual acrobatics of sorts - plugged into entangled wires and software. What can better express the manageability and marketing of art? Neither China nor India offer a market for modern art, while the Western-oriented Soviet Union allows some acceptance of it despite its state-controlled "socialist realism."

Our identification of capitalism with a particular and unique mind-set vis à vis entities implicitly connected the present Western self-understanding with an idea all too familiar to any anthropologist: the homo faber idea of man as tool and work man. And with this, we also implied that all knowledge that aims at the technical control and the mastery of entities is given priority over all religious knowledge of salvation and philosophy. Indeed, the rapidly growing knowledge of control as employed in technology has begun to permeate areas in which it, at best, should play only a minimal role.

The tendency to bring whatever things under excessive human control shows itself, for instance, in phenomena like political liberation theology, which, on the basis of a pursuit of social justice, seeks to make both the salvation and the faith of a human being dependent upon bringing under control social conditions. Conditional calculation with salvation of this kind would not be thinkable in Hindu, Buddhist, or Islamic experiences of what may serve here as Divine. They do not allow of establishing a relation between work and any priest activism, on the one hand, and of faith, on the other. Instead, the core of their religious experience - sometimes not distinguishable from metaphysical experience - is self-communion in silence. This is all the more important for us to be mentioned as the poverty levels in parts of Africa, Asia, and the Near East - where these religions are at home - are by far lower than those in Latin American countries where the Christian liberation theology is practiced, leading one to think that Eastern religious leaders could long ago have developed a system of their own comparable to liberation activisms. But neither work ethics nor excessive desires to control entities allow of any execution of such activities in their sketch of self understanding; nor does any expansionism of controls of things in nature. Indeed, liberation theology is hardly known in those parts of the globe and when it is seen in action, it is understood to be a typical Western, capitalizing institution because of its implicit endeavors to bring something under control Western style, i.e., with a relative disregard of salvation.

Much has been written on the impact of knowledge of control and all technical knowledge in education. The identification of education with information by way of the use of technical means such as computers, calculators, and other devices reveals the very controlling influence on education by outside means. No doubt, the benefit of computer knowledge cannot be overestimated in areas like medicine, physics, or international exchange of information, be it political or economical. But technology does overstep its borders in the area of education. The first signs are already clearly visible in the growing loss of memory capacities in children due to their growing dependence on computer information they learn to handle in school. The computer in education is increasingly substituting both mnemonic exercises and creative, contextual thinking and imagination indispensible for the mental growth of the child and adolescent. Already this one factor alone has lead to a growing generation gap, which, if not remedied, might have severe consequences in the near future that can at best be evaluated in psychiatry and psychotherapy. Mnemonic loss is evidenced in the present adolescent view that to know how to control the corrector keys on the computer is more effective knowledge than that of learning how to spell as the older generations did. The ominous argument can be extended into other areas such as logarithms, fractions, roots, etc.

A most horrifying example of excessive knowledge of control may be artificial intelligence (AI), which, as the term indicates, is an attempted duplication of human intelligence, but with the addition of unbelievably fast process speeds in clock-time. Despite its fair amount of success, AI is also subject to skepticism by its own experts. They doubt whether the fifth stage of the development of AI, the forthcoming "fifth generation" stage as it is called, will work the way more optimistic experts are hoping it will. Up till now, AI systems are only limited controls over "patterns" of words. They are not in control of contextual, especially everyday, speech, let alone are they in control of intonations that spawn specific meanings as conjoined with phases of absolute time. AI can only handle patterns of words that are embedded in the clock-time programmed by the expert. All AI is a device of what "comes-to-be," to be strictly distinguished from the self-becoming that we discussed earlier. And what comes-to-be in AI rests on the logical if-then, not a what-if relation. No AI has the character of self-becoming and, therefore, the ontological limit of AI must be seen in the absolute time of contextual imagination. The term "creating" in creating programs, or "God" for a perfected AI, is probably an index of technological resentment showing that knowledge of essence and of salvation, unattainable to the predominantly technical person, has been crushed by knowledge of control, which is substituted for it.

What is for us most relevant in a determination of the execution of capitalism as a result of the homo faber sketch is a factor that by far goes beyond the ethos of controlability and manageability: profit. All entities are potential targets of profit. The mind-set does not care whether energy is imported from the Soviet Union into Europe or whether it is tapped from the sun and transferred to America. Profit is at the core of knowledge of control. In order to elucidate this proposition, we have to once more return to the notion of the idea as sketch.

d) A Second Look at the Idea as Sketch and the Essence of Capitalism and Economics

Technical control of entities alone does not circumscribe the essence of capitalism. For the tendency toward technical control of things is as old as mankind. It can be found in ancient, so-called primitive cultures and can be traced back to the earliest signs of human existence. In this sense, man is tool-man, homo faber. Nevertheless, such a tendency never had the overwhelming character as it has today. When the primitive man sought control of entities, he availed himself of his will, of invocations, etc., and not of technical means only. He believed firmly in all sorts of magic powers, and in his will to be able to turn entities like rain, harvest, disease, etc., into wished-for directions. In this sense, even the Indian psychic techniques mentioned earlier are also tendencies to bring the self under control for temporary extinction.

In all purely volitional tendencies to change events, however, there was one element missing, or, at best, hardly conspicuous: profit. The concept of profit lies at the very end of a long historical development of the tendencies toward controls of entities. In tandem with this long historical development is the human will, which is necessarily tied up with all controlling tendencies.

For our purposes, the history of the will may briefly be summed up in terms of the role the will plays in our individual lives. In Part I, section b, we discussed the "shifts" of the dimensions of the past, present, and future in absolute time. It is within this dynamic structure that the development of the will has its obvious place. For in the younger periods of our lives, the will does not only aim at what is feasible, but often toward what is not feasible and cannot be realized in the infinite horizon of the future. The young, idealistic person might "will" to change the course of all history, knowing full well - but not quite admitting to himself - that he cannot succeed. This pertains to primitive man as he tried to "will" rain, harvest, and even will to shun tragedy. Any will directed to the impossible betrays a youthful, vivid, and active imagination. But during the later years of our lives, the very scope of what we think is willable narrows and contracts to only what, in reality, can be willed. "Be realistic," the father might advise his young, idealistic son who tries to change the world. In mid-age, the human will is forced into a growing compromise between willing the impossible and what can be willed in practice. The diminution of the scope of the will is a factor oftentimes ignored in therapies of mid-life crises. This diminution forces the person to set the stakes of his will backward and closer to what is possible to be willed. This, in turn, generates feelings of disappointment, frustration, discontent, powerlessness. The latter may spawn feelings of resentment to be found among mid-age and elderly people showing signs of envy of the young who still believe in the impossible or pretend to be able to realize this will.

The contraction of the scope of what can be willed is, however, compensated by the growing concern for acquisitions, gains, and accumulation of things, which can be extracted from things remaining in the narrowed scope of the will. The original youthful and phantasmic goals of the will narrow down into a fixation of profits sought in what is left for the will to realize. Literary figures such as the elderly miser (Molière), the Scrooge (Dickens), and the witches of fairy tales are the best illustrations for this aspect of growing age. This person-type, male or female, does not without reason stand out for what he is and does in all cultures. Not infrequently, he becomes a tragic figure when the time has come for him to draw up a will, surrendering all those acquisitions and profits to others, but with a certain pull in his hand, saying, "Why not postpone it for now at least?" A contracted scope of the will is conjoined with the appearance of entities as capital. This character of entities is very different from early stages in our lives when things are experienced in a more lived, organismic fashion. A young girl experiences her doll as alive. In her mind-set, she is her mother and the doll is her, being given all the attention that her actual mother may not have given or attention that is wished for by the actual child. The doll is no plastic merchandise to the young girl, but "speaks" to her. The capital-character of entities only appears as the girl matures. This does not, however, exclude the fact that through education, public opinion, etc., the young person can become precociously old by being trained into the capitalizing of entities. Indeed, this is what is happening today. And there is already one clear-cut effect of this: the more a young person is exposed to the capitalization of things only, the more the ability of youthful enjoyment and joviality is replaced by aged demeanor and a lack of smiles. He is more and more in need of artificial, technical means to find pleasures and enjoyment to cover up the loss of carefree youth and easy contentment. He strives for more and more technical means to reach contentment, but which, in the end, do not replace the joviality lost too early. The role model of the young "entrepeneur" reveals traces of this.

A key passage in Scheler's ethics, written prior to 1913, may be quoted here. The passage has vast ranges of applicability in today's tendencies to find enjoyment through artifical means of all kinds and sometimes to find them at all costs: "Indeed, one can say that the number of means designed to produce pleasure and to remove sensible pain (e.g. narcotics) increases as unhappiness and negativity in vital feeling become the inner fundamental attitude of a society."[8]

Before taking up the phenomenon of profit as essential to capitalism, we will take a second look at the essence of a "sketch." Our talk of the capitalistic sketch of man of himself remains in need of more clarification for the understanding of capitalism as a primary execution in the self-sketch of contemporary man.

There has been a difficulty up to this point that has not been spelled out. This difficulty consists in the fact that it must actually be impossible to speak of a sketch as we did in Part III. For while doing so, we were already ourselves within a presketched sketch that was not articulated during our explanations. When I am looking at a table and see it under the aspects of beauty or profit, it is presupposed that in each case an antecedent sketch is already there for this to now do. All consciousness must be attitudinal, and therefore, must be continuously sketching.

Precisely this lies in the essence of a sketch, both in the sense of an idea of the mind, as well as in the sense of a sketch of our own personality. Every human being possesses an image of himself, an image that he strives to be at every moment of his actions. From this image - no matter how covertly it may have been functioning from our early days on - there ensue all executions of our actions. If our actions deviate from it, we immediately feel a disparity in us, telling us: "There was something wrong with me." The essence of our self-sketch, or the ways we sketch ourselves, lies in the unfinished and becoming outlines, which themselves remain variable during our sketching. A sketch is, in essence, something unfinished from the start and not only in the everyday sense of being unfinished because it was not completed. All sketches of ourselves are unfinished from the beginning because a sketch sketches in variable and not fixed lines, just as any execution of it admits of numerous variations as we saw, remaining indebted to the original, unfinished starting points of the sketch within which executions take place. Human self-understanding, individual or collective, is contained "in" the process of variable self-sketching, which remains un- or subconscious. Any sketch of ourselves is as invisible as its executions through actions that cover it up. As we saw, executions cover up the essence of a sketch, as it is illustrated throughout the arts. If Beethoven had himself executed the rough sketches he made of his tenth symphony, its execution performed by the conductor would have realized, it is true, the tenth symphony as real. But the original sketch would have been covered up, although it remains variably translucent in all execution. Hence, it is paradoxical to say that a sketch, unfinished, unexecuted, or in this case unperformed, is richer than a more completed sketch. But this paradox lies in the very essence of a sketch. And since any sketch allows of more than one execution, we can never even know whether there is one execution that is congruent with its original sketch.

This state of affairs is part and parcel of art. Whenever a painter "roughs out" a painting, he does not have in his mind and imagination the completed work of art aimed at. The first lines he draws out are not placed within an already perfect whole. The latter is the case only in craft. A tailor cuts a jacket after a fixed pattern. All cuts must be fitted into this pattern. But the artist's lines do not fit fixed patterns. Rather, they play within a pattern qua sketch and are therefore unfinished. The execution of the artist's sketch freely flows out from the sketch and leaves behind the original sketch, piece by piece. The artist "creates" in sketching by letting his hand freely glide over the canvas or paper, at times only in trying or attempting fashion. And each phase of execution and of sketching is in tandem with the meaning of the sketch and with the phases of executions in absolute time.

The variable relationship between executions and sketch, the variable relationship between human executions of actions and the sketch of self (or the idea of oneself), now explains that human beings, at any indivisible moment, never know who they are in that indivisible moment in their own personal nature. At best, they only know who and what they have just been, or what they looked like in the more distant clock-time.[9] We do not know who we are at this moment - which has now already passed away - because of the unfinishedness of the initial lines of our self-sketch happening at any moment. Our sketch must first pass over, in absolute time, to its functionalization with reality. It can do so only because its terminus ad quo, its inception, is replete with possibilities of executions, of which one or the other may more or less realize the original sketch of our own lives.

Since it is impossible to know any initial points of our self-sketch, it is equally impossible to come up with a fixed definition of the present self-understanding of man, or with an "idea of man," such that it would bring us into a position of determining which executions would likely be happening in the near future. All we can do is to ask from typical executions back into the type of sketching from which they come and stem. The human self-sketch is no object that can be observed in space. All we can hope for at this point is to determine the direction the relationship of man and entities is taking in absolute time, a direction toward a future that becomes in the present sketch of self and world. And the executions accessible to us tell us that this unfinished relationship is presently characterized by domination, control, manageability, and the capitalization of entities. These appear to be the common characters in the thick strokes of political and economic executions of man's capitalist self-sketch. Keeping in line with our subject matter, we will focus on the latter, on the capitalization of entities. This, however, implies elucidation of a phenomenon without which capitalism in its meaning given is not thinkable: the phenomenon of profit.

In Part II, section b, we saw that the three major drives play a part in historical development. We distinguished three phases in history, characterized by the prevalence of one of these drives. Firstly, during the early phases of history, the drive of procreation prevailed with concomitant tendencies for domination over human beings. Secondly, this phase was followed by the prevalence of the power drive with concomitant tendencies of domination over both human beings and things. This phase, we stated, culminated, after millenia of slow but steady increase, in the power struggle during the past centuries. It is now beginning to decline. Thirdly, the drive of nutrition is emerging as a prevailing drive, ensuing a tendency of the mind toward domination over things in nature only. That is, the future age will be one of economics and technology, taken in the widest meaning of these terms.

Since power struggles are still going on in the present, one can, nevertheless, realize an increasing tendency of avoiding global conflict in favor of negotiations and endeavors seeking compromise. History, we said with Max Scheler, will become "less historical" with the new attitude toward controls over entities only and the profit that can be gained from them, rather than controls primarily over human beings (wars of conquest). War is seen as less and less "profitable." As seen from the dynamic theory of drives, we are presently living in an age of transition in which power struggles are still lingering on, but the relentless control over things in nature has already begun.

The reason why any theory of the roles of drives in history sounds more or less far-fetched today is that investigations into these roles have been neglected in our time. Indeed, human beings tend to neglect the functions of their own various drives, which, too, undergo three major shifts in our lifetime: youth, maturity, and old age. Taking these phases as a basis, one can state that in each of them there takes place a subtle shift in the interests we take in the entities around us as well as in the attitude and mind-sets by which we perceive entities.

During puberty, the perspectives of our interests are different from those in maturity, which, in turn, are different in old age.

There is no doubt that the shifts of the prevalence of drives, as well as of the aforementioned shifts in the role of the human will, are intrinsically connected with the shifts of the dimensions of the past, the present, and the future in absolute time, which we discussed in Part I. We are of the opinion that in any analysis of historical prediction these shifts must be taken into account. This is especially necessary when a generalization of the shifts in an individual life into life in general is made. O. Spengler generalized these shifts, although in different context, into wholes of cultures and civilizations, saying that they have their youth, their climax, and their decline. Much as his theory has been criticized, it has neither been disproven nor ever been shown to be an unlikely theory that could not stand the test of practical experience and evidence. It may look as if we, too, are going too far by injecting our three drive phases into all life as a whole, having its own terrestrial phases of origins, climax, and decline. But we would also be going too far if we conceived life developing only in linear fashion into infinity, having no origins, climax, and decline. It is much more acceptable to conceive life and its stages and phases in a circular fashion, allowing of ups and downs, of the birth and death of civilizations as well as of the reemergence of new life. In this way, a metaphysics of life would indicate that life as a whole survives its internal stages of growth and decline as does a tree whose leaves come and go with periods of seasons; and the question whether "life itself" is, or is not, subject to the fate of these phases would be one of pure philosophy, and in conjunction with it, of religious faith and science.

I make brief mention of the above factors because they point to a metaphysics of economics and technology in that the nature of absolute time must be understood before one can "project" into the future. For all the shifts of phases, individual or collective, happen in the form of transitions in and of absolute time. This pertains to both the individual life and to life as whole.

Our suggestion that the future of mankind will largely be determined by the hidden forces of the drive of nutrition finally allows us to focus on the essence of economic capitalism: possession and profit.

It is not capitalism, but the drive of nutrition, that is the foundation of "possession." It belongs to the makeup of an organism that, during the intake of food, edibles become the possession of respective organs and of the organism as a whole. As soon as food occupies organic surfaces, such as tongue and gum, it takes possession of these organs and vice versa. Possession, therefore, is not a notion in the mind only, but is based on the intrinsic vital experience in any organism.

One can describe the genesis of possession in the following manner. An infant taking in his mother's milk has no "idea" of the milk. On the basis of what has been said earlier, the infant has an "image" in the phantasy of the nutritive drive. It is only after two years or so that the infant not only learns to make distinctions between himself and others around him (emergence of the will),[10] but also that the determinability of his growing mind functionalizes with the image in the phantasy of this particular drive, and begins to sketch (the idea of) possession of what has been taken in. This sketching occurs in absolute time and represents the transition between image and idea and idea and image.

After this functionalization, the concept of possession becomes applicable throughout the child's future life in ever so many executions in reality. Possession, therefore, is not a direct outcome of social conditions. Even in a utopian society having neither classes nor possessions that could set human beings apart - a notion, by the way, that has again and again been courted by extreme leftists and other simpletons since the nineteenth century - neither the possessions of food nor the expressions of basic instinctive behavior, such as the green-eyed look at someone else's food, or, for that matter, the latter's overreacting to someone else getting too close to his food, could ever be eliminated. If there is one drive that, for better or for worse, sets human beings and animals apart, it is the drive of nutrition and its objective bread basket.

It is not the nutritive drive and possession alone, however, that functionalizes the idea of capitalism and economics. This functionalization occurs with equal force with the accumulative drive, or the drive of hoarding and collecting, i.e., the drive that we refer to as the "gathering drive." All accumulation, including its widely spread occurrence throughout the animal world, cannot be thought or explained without this drive of gathering entities. All profit-taking in capitalism belongs to accumulation. What is accumulated or gathered is done so in the name of profit. While too much accumulation may inflate or devalue profit, and, conversely, too little of it may increase values beyond their reach, the art of economics consists, in part at least, in hitting the delicate balance between these extremes. It is well known that this balance is not a fixed one, but changes along with the psychology of a market, a changing feel of expectations, or with the optimitic or pessimistic outlooks from areas well outside economics, like the end of a century.

In order to appreciate the delicacy of this balance, often taken for granted as a simple fact, I wish to draw attention to the phenomenon of gathering itself - at the heart of economics - as can be found in pure philosophy. The brief description following by no means fully covers all of the essence of the phenomenon concerned.

All of nature is imbued with the phenomenon of gathering. As all instances of gathering show us, gathering gathers itself by engendering its own limits or boundaries beyond which no further gathering takes place. The winds whirling autumn leaves around and around down the street allow so many and no more leaves to be gathered in them. The leaves will soon stop whirling and are dispersed. Just as the gathering of leaves thusly comes to an end in itself, so also does the gathering of all instances of the kind, like tornadoes or eddies. Animals, too, gather and hoard foods for the winter, but only up to a point. They do not keep on storing indefinitely. Of course, new winds might pick up leaves, again blowing them down the street, and the animal might also resume storing; but, in the end, all gathering gathers itself to an end. It reaches a maximum. When such maxima are reached, whatever was gathered, and the gathering itself, falls apart and collapes. At this point, it can be seen that enduring gathering must stay under its inherent maximum. If the whole world would be seen as an immense gathering, its lasting existence could not allow of reaching a maximum.

The phenomenon of gathering shows us, then, that throughout nature instances of gathering reveal a measure beyond which nothing more is and should be gathered together. As it is well known, the meaning of "gathering" is central to the ancient Greek Logos. The word Logos is, as we have stated, derived from the Greek legein, which means "to gather" or "to collect." In this original meaning of Logos, there is, like in the Chinese Tao, implied the quintessence of "measure" beyond which nothing more is gatherable. When the Greeks conceived man as the very bearer of this Logos, man himself was seen as the measure of all things (Protagoras).[11] When, on the other hand, the Logos was seen in its own purity of its gathering itself (Heraclitus), the measure of Logos was seen intrinsic to it. Even the sun, gathering for us all visible things, had its measure by not being allowed to step over its own domain. Ultimately, however, the measure of Logos consisted in the harmony that holds all opposites, e.g., hot-cold, dark-bright, together in gathering them, just as the harmony of a melody holds the discrete and opposing sounds, chords, and tones together.

Heidegger was quite right in stressing that Logos and Harmony mean the same in pre-Socratic thought. But he did not fully look into the phenomenon of gathering itself, at least not to its very end. He did not conjoin this phenomenon with "measure." The measure of gathering, or Logos, is, of course, no measurement, just as Anaxagoras' intuition of a vortex as the gathering of all entities is no measurement. But the Logos and the vortex do have measure in common. The measure of them may best be described as self-restriction, although this is only another word for what is ineffable. Our modern word "logic" is an almost invisible trace of the pre-Socratic meaning of Logos. For modern logic, too, gathers into ordering sets and wholes the terms it speaks of, albeit on the basis of the modern but un-Greek understanding of truth as noncontradiction. But the indigenous meaning of the pre-Socratic Logos was the Presence of gathering of all opposites, including a fortiori those of true and false, and excluding, a fortiori, past and future as thought to be outside the Present (Parmenides). It is Presence itself that gives here the limit and the measure to the gathering of opposites. When Parmenides, for instance, insists that Being is "limited" and "full," he may have had precisely this in view.

The modern accumulative gathering taking place in technology and economics, however, is separated by an abyss from the above description of the phenomenon of gathering. It is irreconcilable with the measure in gathering, let alone with ancient Greek Logos or Chinese Tao, both of which contain the phenomenon of gathering in their respective grasp of Being. But capitalist gathering has the grotesque character of crossing over and overstepping the boundaries of its own sketch. Storing or gathering is another thick stroke in the sketch of the capitalist world because it crosses over and beyond the sketch of gathering. Entities are gathered, stored, and accumulated beyond conceivable maxima. Oversupplies and surpluses indicate that a balance has been missed and that it can only be restored in permissible degrees if retribution is paid to diminish them (subsidies, etc.).

But other retributions - a term I borrow from the pre-Socratic thinker Anaximander - can occur, and seemingly independent of man's controls, in the form of opposites of surpluses: deficits. While surpluses and deficits should play within boundaries of possible measures in the phenomenon of gathering, they must not fall outside such measures, that is, they should play within the sketch of gathering. This is neither to blame capitalism nor capitalist socialism alone for excessive and endless gathering within their own possibilities of doing so. It appears that all humans themselves experience, at least in some periods of their lives, excessive gathering. But whatever they may gather in terms of possessions, monies, remembrances, experiences, beliefs, acquaintances, friendships, etc., begins at some crucial point to weigh on them, becoming a personal gravity, if you will, on their shoulders, a growing gravity saying, "Look what you have done and accomplished, and now you must carry it all." This gravity of gathered accumulations suffuses all classes among humans, ranging from the multimillionaire, who feels the "growing pains" of his endlessly growing wealth, which does not necessarily make him happy, to the homeless person succumbing somewhere in the street to the excessive weight of a dozen or so plastic bags filled to the brim with gathered stuff. Like scattered leaves in the street after their gathering winds have subsided, here, too, in the human realm, gathering comes to exhaust itself.

The psychological motive for the present fascination and frequent obsession with computer and other push-button devices lies in the fact that the respective industry has immensely helped the individual to expand the limits and measures of storing and gathering, and thereby immensely expanding their manageability. In this respect, the computer is an irreplaceable asset for profit and advantage in all areas that are tailored to computer investigation. In our context, however, there is also another view of the computer. As a gathering device collecting and utilizing in split seconds huge amounts of data vastly surpassing the mind's grasp of such amounts in such a short time, it is also a device strongly associated with what has passed. And this is its shortcoming over against the mind. That is, whatever is gathered and stored (memory) by a computer pertains to either what has already just passed, or to what already lies in a more distant past. A computer cannot store out of the future, much as the computer is, as a technological device, of the future. These distinctions are glossed over in evaluating the industry's potential. The computer has only a very limited relation to the future. At best, its application to predictability lies in computer graphics; that is, it pertains to spatial objects or to those that admit of graphic spatialization on the screen. Our example of planting a tree so that at some future time it will cast shade on a certain area of the backyard showed that spatial objects are easier to predict than purely temporal ones. The temporal objects, we stated, can be predicted relatively well only in terms of statistics, but with respective margins of error, which, however, are also sometimes very large. Since the computer is itself a spatial object, it would not seem to be possible for it to predict much more than what is predictable in space. And here, it seems, the prediction is short-term, both in terms of clock-time and in terms of meaning. A computer graphic may show the electrical activity of brain cells indicating a predictability of the direction a limb will be moved within a split second. But the same graphic does not, and cannot, show the intention of the moving of a limb and subsequent different movements.

The computer is bare of contextual phantasy and imagination through which things like intentions functionalize themselves with real factors in life and our historical situation that is interfaced with the intentions of others gathered in such situations. In short, any computer is bare of impulsion and absolute time, which are the conditions for any creative imagination in prediction.

The unquestionable advantage and profit accumulated by the efficiency of the computer at the end of our century is contributing to a sketch of the world resembling a chessboard that is infinitely spread out in space. Its chessmen, i.e., entities, are to be moved back and forth, and preferably by logical rules to produce advantage and profit, and more advantage and more profit, not only in the material sense of these terms. It is for the sake of profit that any and all entities may fall, no matter whether king, queen, or pawn: anything can fall on this chessboard for the sake of useful profit, including the measure in the gathering itself of data.

As seen through a Franciscan mind-set, which can be considered to be an extreme but viable alternative to the capitalist mind-set in that it would be filled with humility, thankfulness, happiness in privation, modesty, love of God,[12] terms like gathering, accumulation, storing, collecting, the artifical meaning of "memory," etc., are only a few different expressions among the hellborn elements in the excessive execution of the sketch of capitalism and its mind-set. In it, gathering has become tantamount to capitalization. And capitalization suffuses all walks of life, sports as well as economics, educational "programs" as well as art and religion, science as well as politics. On this chessboard of the capitalist mind-set, entities derive significance and relevance only from their calculability and capitalizability. The relentless search and craving for capitalization beyond the measure of gathering has begun even to subordinate the human person, and its functionalization with life, to artificial intelligence extracted from brain functions and process patterns.

Let a linguistic observation bring our study to a close. The term "profit" implies advance without end. The Latin proficere or proficisci means: to make headway, to advance without end or limit. Profectus means growth. These words were absorbed in English usage in the fourteenth century and belong to the historical origins of modern capitalism.

By contrast, the term "finance" is derived from the Latin finis, which means "end," "goal," "aim." Finis has, therefore, the same meaning as the Greek telos. The Greek word telos also meant "taxes," "customs" (teloi). Our word "finances" goes back to this ancient Greek usage. Literally, the word "finance," or the word "finances" (finis, fines), means re-fine-ment of entities (monies), whereas "profit" projects an endless, linear progress of whatever useful accumulation and gathering. As a Roman equivalent to the Greek telos, the word "finance" echoes the Greek measure in gathering, whereas "profit" does not. This may be part of the historical reason why profits and their losses are always in disagreement with the measured refinement of finance that portrays them.

NOTES

PART I

1. See Martin Heidegger, HERAKLIT. GESAMTAUSGABE Vol. 55, Manfred S. Frings, ed. (Vittorio Klosterman: Frankfurt a.M. 1979), p. 135.

2. See Max Scheler, "The Psychology of So-called Compensation Hysteria and the Real Battle against Illness," E. Vacek, S.J., trans., in: JOURNAL OF PHENOMENOLOGICAL PSYCHOLOGY, Vol. 15, 2, 1984.

3. Heraclitus, Fragment DK: 88. The same thought of exchanges can be found in Chuang Tzu (ca. 300 B.C.) almost verbatim.

4. Concerning the distinction between non-being and relative non-being, see M. Frings Nothingness and Being," in PHENOMENOLOGICAL RESEARCH, pp. 183f., 1979; and "Max Scheler. Vom Sein des Dinges in wissenssoziologischer Sicht," Proceedings of the XI World Congress of Philosophy, Vol. 5, Sophia 1975, pp. 691-695.

5. See Max Scheler SPÄTE SCHRIFTEN, Collected German Edition, Vol. 9, Manfred S. Frings, ed. (Francke Verlag: Berne, 1976.

NOTES

PART II

1. I. Kant, CRITIQUE OF PURE REASON, A 220. B 268.

2. See Max Delbrück, MIND FROM MATTER (Palo Alto: Blackwell, 1986), esp. pp. 31ff.

3. Delbrück's biogenetic theory of perception possesses valuable implications for the phenomenology of perception (Husserl, Merleau-Ponty, Scheler) of which Delbrück seemingly was not aware.

4. The term "impulsion" is rendered from the German word "Drang," for which there is no precise equivalent in English. "Drang" has sometimes been rendered as "urge" or "basic drive," which are nearly synonymous, but do not cover the German meaning of the word. As a word in everyday German use, "Drang" implies a strong albeit impeded desire, yearning, or tendency. Being caught in a traffic jam, for instance, there is a "Drang" to get off at the nearest exit or to wait it out until the jam has cleared up. In German classical literature, the phrase "Sturm und Drang" is not covered in the English translation of "Storm and Stress." For in both German literature and the philosophy of life, "Drang" implies a continuous impediment. In particular, in the dynamic theory of reality (Bouterweck, Dilthey, Duns Scotus, Fichte, Jacobi, Maine de Biran, Scheler, Schelling, Schopenhauer), all existence is given in a continous factor of impediment, resistance implicit in "Drang." Any "impulse" (organic, psychic, emotive, volitional, mental, or even existential) is possible only in the resistance of what the impulse is progressing toward, or, conversely, without impulse (or impulsion in general) no reality can be given or posited. Reality, therefore, is neither the outcome of consciousness nor of perception. Reality is given first in the subconscious, vital factor of the capacity to resist:"Drang."

NOTES

PART III

1. Scheler was already familiar with Heidegger's concept of "at-handedness" when he read Heidegger's BEING AND TIME. For details see my analyses of the possibility of ethics in BEING AND TIME on the basis Scheler's Value-Ethics, PERSON UND DASEIN, (The Hague: Martinus Nijhoff: Phaenomenologica, 32, 1969), pp. 38-44.

2. Concerning "psychic contagion" see; Max Scheler. THE NATURE OF SYMPATHY, trans. Peter Heath (Hamden: Shoe String Press, 1973), Part I, 2.

3. PHILOSOPHISCHE ANTHROPOLOGIE, GESAMMELTE WERKE, Vol. 12, Manfred S. Frings, ed., (Bonn: Bouvier Verlag, 1987), p. 148f.

4. Max Scheler, ON THE ETERNAL IN MAN, trans. Bernhard Noble (Hamden: Shoe String Press, 1972), pp. 199-203. The indices of subjects in the German Collected Edition list many more references to "functionalization." Conf. especially, Vol. 12, loc. cit., p. 146.

5. FORMALISM IN ETHICS AND NON-FORMAL ETHICS OF VALUES, trans. Manfred S. Frings and Roger L. Funk (Evanston: Northwestern University Press, 1973), p. 12.

6. I pointed to the significance of the temporality of moral goodness first in my Introduction (Einleitung) to Pope Paul John II, philosohical writings, in Karol Wojtyla Johannes Paul II. PRIMAT DES GEISTES. PHILOSOPHISCHE SCHRIFTEN (Stuttgart: Seewald Verlag, 1980), pp. 19-33. I regard the temporality of the moral good as a most pressing problem in ethics today, and I have referred to it on other occasions in various details. Scheler never articulated moral temporality in his work, but must

be credited for having paved an important way toward this question in the foundation of ethics.

7. METAPHYSIK UND ERKENNTIS, GESAMMELTE WERKE, Vol. 11, Manfred S. Frings, ed., (Berne and Munich: Francke Verlag, 1979), pp. 119f. This fragment was written in 1926/7.

NOTES

PART IV

1. Martin Heidegger, HERAKLIT, op. cit., pp. 186-199.

2. The following clarification of the concept of capitalism is based on a manuscript by Max Scheler, dated 1919, and recently discovered in Munich. It was published in Vol. 4 of the German Collected Edition, POLITISCH PÄDAGOGISCHE SCHRIFTEN (Essays in Politics and Education) Manfred S. Frings, ed. (Berne and Munich: Francke Verlag, 1982), pp. 615-75. Part of the following explanation of capitalism was published in PHILOSOPHY TODAY, Celina, Ohio, Spring 1986.

3. PHILOSOPHY TODAY, loc. cit., p. 38 and footnote 1.

4. Martin Heidegger, PARMENIDES, GESAMTAUSGABE Vol. 56, Manfred S. Frings, ed., (Frankfurt: Vittorio, Klostermann, 1981), p. 140ff.

5. Max Scheler, SPÄTE SCHRIFTEN, Manfred S. Frings, ed., Berne: Francke Verlag, 1976), p. 145.

6. Martin Heidegger, PARMENIDES, pp. 25-30; 104-09; 195-208.

7. Max Scheler, FORMALISM IN ETHICS, loc. cit., p. 178.

8. Max Scheler, FORMALISM IN ETHICS, loc. cit., pp. 345-46.

9. Max Scheler, PROBLEMS OF A SOCIOLOGY OF KNOWLEDGE, Manfred S. Frings, trans.; with an Introduction by Kenneth Strikkers (London: Routledge & Kegan Paul, 1982).

10. Max Scheler, THE NATURE OF SYMPATHY, Peter Heath, trans. (London: Routledge & Kegan Paul, Ltd., 1954), Part III.

11. Conf.: M.S. Frings, "Protagoras Rediscovered. Heidegger's Explication of Protagoras' Fragment," THE JOURNAL OF VALUE INQUIRY Vol. VIII, 2, 1974.

12. Conf.: M.S. Frings, "Humility and Existence," DELTA EPSILON SIGMA BULLENTIN, XIX, 4, 174. German trans. in DIE WERTKRISE DES MENSCHEN. PHILOSOPHISCHE ETHIK IN DER HEUTIGEN WELT. FESTSCHRIFT FÜR HANS REINER. (Meisenheim: Verlag Anton Hain, 1979). See also: PHILOSOPHY TODAY, loc. cit., p. 39.

MARTINUS NIJHOFF PHILOSOPHY LIBRARY

1. D. Lamb, Hegel – From Foundation to System. 1980. ISBN 90-247-2359-0
2. I.N. Bulhof, Wilhelm Dilthey: A Hermeneutic Approach to the Study of History and Culture. 1980. ISBN 90-247-2360-4
3. W.J. van der Dussen, History as a Science. The Philosophy of R.G. Collingwood. 1981. ISBN 90-247-2453-8
4. M. Chatterjee, The Language of Philosophy. 1981. ISBN 90-247-2372-8
5. E.-H.W. Kluge, The Metaphysics of Gottlob Frege. An Essay in Ontological Reconstruction. 1980. ISBN 90-247-2422-8
6. D. Dutton and M. Krausz (eds.), The Concept of Creativity in Science and Art. 1981. ISBN 90-247-2418-X
7. F.R. Ankersmit, Narrative Logic. A Semantic Analysis of the Historian's Language. 1983. ISBN 90-247-2731-6
8. T.P. Hohler, Imagination and Reflection: Intersubjectivity. Fichte's *Grundlage* of 1794. 1982. ISBN 90-247-2732-4
9. F.J. Adelmann (ed.), Contemporary Chinese Philosophy. 1982. ISBN 90-247-3057-0
10. E.N. Ostenfeld, Forms, Matter and Mind. Three Strands in Plato's Metaphysics. 1982. ISBN 90-247-3051-1
11. J.T.J. Srzednicki, The Place of Space and Other Themes. Variations on Kant's First Critique. 1983. ISBN 90-247-2844-4
12. D. Boucher, Texts in Context. Revisionist Methods for Studying the History of Ideas. 1985. ISBN 90-247-3121-6
13. Y. Yovel, Nietzsche as Affirmative Thinker. 1986. ISBN 90-247-3269-7
14. M.H. Mitias (ed.), Possibility of the Aesthetic Experience. 1986. ISBN 90-247-3278-6
15. P.E. Langford, Modern Philosophies of Human Nature. 1986. ISBN 90-247-3370-7
16. K. Galloway Young, Taleworlds and Storyrealms. 1987. ISBN 90-247-3415-0
17. W. Horosz, Search Without Idols. 1987. ISBN 90-247-3327-8
18. R. Ellis, An Ontology of Consciousness. 1986. ISBN 90-247-3349-9
19. M.C. Doeser, J.N. Kraay (eds.), Facts and Values. 1986. ISBN 90-247-3384-7
20. M.S. Frings, Philosophy of Prediction and Capitalism. 1987. ISBN 90-247-3542-4
21. S.J. Bartlett and P. Suber (eds.), Self-Reference. 1987. ISBN 90-247-3474-6
22. P. Simpson, Goodness and Nature. 1987. ISBN 90-247-3477-0
23. I. Leman-Stefanovic, The Event of Death: A Phenomenological Enquiry. 1987. ISBN 90-247-3414-4
24. V. Tejera, Nietzsche and Greek Thought. 1987. ISBN 90-247-3475-4
25. S. Satris, Ethical Emotivism. 1987. ISBN 90-247-3413-4
26. J.W. Bernauer, S.J., Amor Mundi. 1987. ISBN 90-247-3483-5
29. H.A. Durfee, Foundational Reflections. 1987. ISBN 90-247-3504-1

Series ISBN 90-247-2344-2